First published by O Books, 2008
O Books is an imprint of John Hunt Publishing Ltd., The Bothy, Deershot Lodge, Park Lane, Ropley,
Hants, SO24 0BE, UK
office1@o-books.net
www.o-books.net

Distribution in:

UK and Europe
Orca Book Services
orders@orcabookservices.co.uk
Tel: 01202 665432 Fax: 01202 666219
Int. code (44)

USA and Canada
NBN
custserv@nbnbooks.com
Tel: 1 800 462 6420 Fax: 1 800 338 4550

Australia and New Zealand
Brumby Books
sales@brumbybooks.com.au
Tel: 61 3 9761 5535 Fax: 61 3 9761 7095

Far East (offices in Singapore, Thailand,
Hong Kong, Taiwan)
Pansing Distribution Pte Ltd
kemal@pansing.com
Tel: 65 6319 9939 Fax: 65 6462 5761

South Africa
Alternative Books
altbook@peterhyde.co.za
Tel: 021 555 4027 Fax: 021 447 1430

Text copyright Gethin Abraham-Williams 2008

Design: Stuart Davies

ISBN: 978 1 84694 149 8

A CIP catalogue record for this book is available
from the British Library.

Printed by Digital Book Print

Spirituality
or Religion?

Do we have to choose?

Gethin Abraham-Williams

BOOKS

Winchester, UK
Washington, USA

CONTENTS

Spirituality or Religion: Do we have to choose?

'Gethin Abraham-Williams' writings always have the capacity to surprise because his insights are always new and fresh on topics which one thought everything possible had already been said. His observations are never trite; he uses no clichés but touches on the things that really matter when one is trying to be a disciple of Jesus. Here is a book that will stretch our minds and imaginations and also move our hearts so that we might better serve God and his world.'
Most Revd Dr Barry Morgan, Archbishop of Wales

'I have known the author for nearly 40 years and our strong friendship is rooted in the mutual fascination of our spiritual diversity. Gethin is often more generous in judging sensitive issues; he adventurously opens doors of thinking which I am content to leave closed; we are both bridge builders, but he is a visionary for new possibilities when I don't see the purpose. So my warm commendation of this book is rather like my friendship with Gethin. It is a generous and adventurous book, destined to carve highways in the desert for travellers seeking uncertain routes to a certain land. The desert trails for travellers at the back of this book are a rich resource - as is the life of the author.'
Rev Dr David Coffey OBE, President of the Baptist World Alliance

'Gethin Abraham-Williams' treatment of the relationship of spirituality and religion is both provocative and inspiring. With fresh insights and profoundly moving examples, he argues that spirituality can be a redeeming response to religion's rigidity and conventionalism. My overwhelming reaction was a desire for further unpacking (maybe a sequel). He gifts the reader with his rich weaving of Scripture, Celtic lore, literary gems, and issues of urgent concern, all serving his belief that religion and spirituality

mutually influence and challenge one another. I recommend this thought-provoking work to anyone who is a disciple and a seeker.'
Sister Joan Puls OSF, American Franciscan and Author

'Do we have to choose between religion and spirituality, asks Gethin Abraham-Williams, in this thoughtful, wide-ranging and generous exploration. No, he argues emphatically, to choose would be disastrous for we need both: compassionate religion, realistic spirituality. Compassion and realism are the hallmarks of this book. Abraham-Williams is sympathetic to those who struggle with religion and who find respite, hope and energy in the new spirituality. He recognises the great strengths of spirituality, and its potential to help us address some of the most pressing issues of the day. But he is also an eloquent apologist for religion, wearing his considerable experience and learning lightly, and calling vividly on anecdote, story and poetry to make his case.

'This is a challenging and provocative book, beneath the warm tone and ready accessibility. At times I felt that we'd be on opposite sides of an argument, but the only real argument would be the unsolvable one about which comes first: religion or spirituality. The more attentively I read, the more it seemed that our meaning and intention are actually very close, it is language that gets in the way. As one who struggles with religion in its institutional manifestation I was particularly struck, and challenged, by the chapter on the relationship between believing and belonging. Ultimately, he argues, belonging encircles believing, because believing is not about holding to a set of propositions, but about trust in God, a God for whom belonging was and always will be unconditional and unlimited. I will carry that challenge with me.'
Eley McAinsh, Director, The Living Spirituality Network and Producer, Something Understood, BBC Radio 4

'This wise, generous and humane book takes the reader on a thoughtful journey into the relationship between religion and spirituality. Ranging across the world's religions, delighting in literature, and open always to the provocation of the Spirit, Gethin Abraham-Williams' study cannot fail to enrich and enlarge our understanding of the ways of God with human beings. All who are interested in contemporary spirituality and religion will benefit from it.'

Revd Dr David Cornick, General Secretary, Churches Together in England and a Fellow of Robinson College, Cambridge

'Gethin Abraham-Williams has made a very helpful contribution to the current debate on religion and spirituality. Rather than see them as simple and unreconcilable opposites, he argues that spirituality is the inner substance to religion, and religion is spirituality's outer and organised expression. The book is packed with insights that will encourage those tempted to give up on religion and 'do their own thing', or those who struggle to connect their own spiritual search with the lives of religious communities. Abraham-Williams is a very fine wordsmith and the book is well and engagingly written, with references to major world religions and the Welsh 'Mabinogion' stories, alongside Christian theology and an excellent range of personal and historical anecdotes from the Christian tradition. I warmly recommend it.'

Revd Dr Robert Ellis, Principal, Regent's Park College, Oxford University

for Denise
whose natural spirituality has always been down to earth

'a fo ben bid bont'
(whoever would lead must first be a bridge)

Cover photograph

It's the startling combination of thugishness and vulnerability in Elizabeth Frink's 'male standing figure' that attracted me to it as a cover photograph for a book that attempts to look at the harsher aspects of the human condition, and of religion's sinister compliance too often in upholding what it should be exposing and condemning. That the figure's head has the appearance of a painted face is significant too, because the sculptor wants us to question what lies beneath the mask. We get a hint of it in eyes that seem more frightened than threatening and nostrils that smell danger rather than convey dominance. In these powerful pieces (it's one of a set) Frink has created a haunting image of disoriented and fallible individuals wanting to be seen as tough. These are figures struggling to deny their spirituality while being aware that they cannot redeem themselves without acknowledging it.

Foreword

The author is one of those rare characters whom once you encounter you are unlikely to forget the experience. In the case of Gethin you are likely, however, to go away with and retain the impression of an enigma. In a remarkable way he combines earnestness with playful and infectious good humour; Christian dedication with a *joie de vivre*. At work he can be either the skilled diplomatist or the contentious provoker as the need arises. Those of us who know him as a friend over many years vouch for his generosity and loyalty.

As a talented and deep thinking Christian minister, he continues as one of the few survivors on the depleted and marginalized liberal wing of the Baptist Denomination. He has had a distinguished career as pastor of key churches in London and the English heartlands, highly valued for his abilities as a preacher and leader. He has recently retired after being for many years the tireless and ubiquitous evangelist for the cause of Christian unity in Wales, sowing and sometimes seeing a harvest appearing in sunless and soil-eroded fields. I know he has had to cope with many a bitter disappointment, yet he has persisted where others would have given up, and succeeded where others would not have thought it even worth a try. Wales owes him an enormous debt.

Sometimes the best way to penetrate a human enigma is to get them to write a book. I hope this may work in the case of Gethin. Psychologists, including amateur psychologists, can have a go at reading between the lines. But many who have not been able to hear his sermons or go around with him on his travels, will now be able to benefit from this experience of Gethin in print. It is a 'Celtic Experience', because his Welshness is more obvious than that of some of us. It is important to realise that to be truly Welsh or Celtic means that knowledge is obtained and shared not simply by means of the intellect alone. We Celts learn in much the same way as some people pray. That's why there is such a close convergence between the currently popular interest in 'Celtic Spirituality' and the 'Spirituality' movement as a whole. Deep calls unto deep! With his conventional Christian upbringing and rigorous academic theological training at Oxford, Gethin is thus well positioned to write a book which strives to bridge the gap between religion and spirituality, a gap which at the present time is gaping wide. This book represents a natural development of Gethin's irrepressible ecumenicity. Religion is in desperate need of spirituality, and spirituality needs the structure and discipline of religion if its refreshing fountains are not to trickle away into the sands. The book is thus addressed to a wide audience, despite the new experience for many of being invited into the dark passages of a Celtic myth. It has an important message for the twenty-first century.

John Henson, *Co-ordinator of 'Good As New', author of 'Other Communions of Jesus', and Greenbelt Speaker*

Preface

Spirituality and religion have fallen out with each other long enough! This book aims to show not only that they need to make up, but why and how. As religion has become progressively self absorbed and spirituality increasingly other worldly, both have failed a generation searching for a vision of a better way. Surprisingly, as religion has become increasingly suspect in popular perception, spirituality has taken off. Many may be reluctant, or even embarrassed to admit to being 'religious', but will often be quite open about their interest in, and pursuit of various forms of spirituality. Why this is so is the subject of the first section. A spirituality that denies, or becomes detached from its religious origins, however, is in danger of ending up with nothing significant to offer, or worse, to substituting a coherent framework of faith with a mishmash of half digested truisms. Equally, when religion denigrates spirituality it denies its own essence, because without a genuine appreciation of spirituality, religion is in danger of losing its soul.

The middle section looks at some significant areas in which religion has been less than effective to the detriment of the common good, and in which spirituality has had to carry the torch. It poses three specific questions: Is there a connection between the fall-off in religious awareness over the last century, and our increasing disregard for the well being of the environment? How can a whole culture become so paralysed that it allows the evil practices it abhors to flourish? And why has religion such a bad record in combating racism when it has also thrown up some heroic figures who have led the crusade for racial equality?

The final section returns to the central thesis of the book with a positive take on religion and spirituality. It argues that religious adherence can be liberating where there is generosity of spirit, because belonging in some form helps believing. It argues that it's possible to be open to people of other faiths without denying the integrity of one's own beliefs, and that engagement with those who see God differently from ourselves enlarges our own understanding of God. The book's final argument is that belief in an afterlife is not 'pie in the sky when you die' but a necessary conviction that sharpens our focus to live responsibly in the here and now.

These themes are played-out in triangular relationships in two arenas. One involves Jesus of Nazareth and the Jewish patriarchs, Moses and Elijah. The other concerns Branwen and her two brothers, Brân and Efnysien, from one of the great folk tales of the Celtic period. Both narratives provide insights that not only complement each other, but challenge our willingness to face uncomfortable truths.

Together they tease and test, sharpen and blur, stretch and squeeze the distinctions between religion and spirituality, and show why it is invidious to expect that we should have to choose between them.

A Splendid Sight:
the Transfiguration according to Luke

'Jesus took Rocky, James and John up a mountain. While Jesus was talking with God, his face looked different, and his white clothes sparkled in the strong light. Suddenly they noticed two people talking to Jesus. These must be the former leaders, Moses and Elijah!! They looked radiant. They were talking about Jesus' coming death in Jerusalem, and how it would bring a new era, like the one Moses brought about. Rocky and his friends were drowsy, but awake enough to see the splendid sight of Jesus and his companions. As the two were leaving, Rocky said to Jesus, "It's great up here, Boss! Let's make three shrines, one for you, one for Moses, and one for Elijah!" Rocky blurted this out without thinking. At that moment, the clouds came down thick on the mountain and gave them the shivers. They heard a voice coming out of the mists, saying, "*This* is my Own, my Chosen; listen to *him*." After the voice, they saw Jesus again, but he was on his own. The friends kept quiet about this experience until sometime afterwards.'

Luke, chapter 9, verses 28 - 36

Good as New: A Radical Retelling of the Scriptures (O Books, 2004)

Branwen's Story:
a Celtic tale with a Gospel meaning

Branwen's story, which forms one of the threads running through this book, is one of the most memorable episodes in the Celtic masterpiece, 'The Mabinogion'. Behind the myth and magic of legend, lies a real world where people struggle to make sense of their circumstances and look for help from a parallel universe to ward off their fears and to make sense of their lives.

In this tale, the courts of Britain and Ireland, ruled respectively by Brân and Matholwch, represent the formalised worlds that are familiar to organised religion. The two nations stand for those things which are good in each, with their respective practices and established rites. From time to time alliances are proposed between them but often thwarted. Hurts received or imagined, result in further misunderstanding or lead to open conflict.

Spirituality's champion is Branwen, the beautiful princess who is Brân's sister and eventually becomes Matholwch's queen. She is the one who seeks to bring about reconciliation when relationships fail, is loved and generates love in others. She is also the one who is most hurt when love is spurned, and eventually dies of a broken heart. It is her spirituality that permeates the story. If Brân eventually emerges as the representative of the forces of good over the forces of evil, it is because Branwen has been his inspiration.

Throughout, evil plays a game with the equivalents of religion and spirituality. Evil's embodiment is Branwen's half brother, the sinister Efnysien, who creates disharmony in the family and between peoples. Thwarted in his need to control and dominate, he turns friends into enemies and turns away the love of those he wants most. At the end even he is convicted by the extent of the suffering he's caused, and dies in a state of contrition.

This and the other stories in 'The Mabinogion', emerged during a particularly uncertain period in the history of Britain. That they still speak to us, and to many other nations in equally uncertain times, is a tribute to the genius of those mediaeval story tellers and their willingness to handle big themes and to set them against the reality of flesh and blood.

To read these stories in all their fascinating detail, see Sioned Davies' translation, 'The Mabingion' (Oxford, 2007). The quotations introducing each section of the book, and in the chapters are all drawn from this contemporary version.

For music inspired by Branwen's Story, listen to '... onyt agoraf y drws... (... unless I open the door ...)' by Guto Pryderi Puw (BBC MM295 Great Prom Premieres)

I

THE DOOR WE MUST NOT OPEN

Y drws ny dylywn ni y agori

1. The Movement of a curtain: religion's eclipse by spirituality

'Fear wist not to evade as Love wist to pursue'

Religion is out and spirituality is in. Maybe. Maybe not. Certainly for Kate, a hospital consultant, religion had become something of a problem. It was buried deep in a letter between friends, as if the admitting was no light thing, but had to be hacked and mined out of the more inaccessible seams of her being. 'I cannot feel comfortable in the Church here,' she revealed. 'It is very routine and unimaginative. Also I begin to feel a bit of a heretic these days – I am a follower of Christ's teaching and philosophy; I believe in a God (a concept I do not find easy or even wish to describe in concrete terms). However, I do not even feel the need for all the complex ideas of "God made man", "redemption", etc. I am comforted to realise that some theologians agree.'

Kate had thinkers in mind like Professor Keith Ward, the popular and respected Christian academic in Oxford, honest enough to say that 'to become Christians, we seem to have to take on board a very complicated philosophy and become involved about angels on the heads of pins,' and 'it is all very confusing and not very relevant.' And there are many more like him, mainstream scholars sensitive to the difficulties created by trying to describe the indescribable and to systematise an awareness of Perfect Being that is best hinted at by means of negative descriptions: 'in-effable', 'in-visible', 'im-mortal'.

For Kate, ever the realist, the theory had to make sense where she was, and the reality didn't match up to the ideology. 'I find it hard to go to Evensong in a little village church, unwilling to say the Creed and bored or irritated by sermons which are irrelevant to me. The Church of England may need more "magic" and "evangelism" for some, but it needs more rational thought for the scientist in me and more relevance philosophically. I thought I might try the Quakers, but lack motivation!' Now working abroad, she had grown up in Britain and belonged to that kind of solid Anglican family that is the backbone of many parish communities, a no-nonsense but sincere and committed Christian.

Nevertheless, even for someone with her background religion was now proving burdensome, and she had worked out a faith position for herself that could be described as semi-detached. There are very many, men as well as women, like her, within as well as outside the practices of the great world religions, for whom spirituality is a lifeline to faith where religion has proved too restrictive and circumscribed. Spirituality has therefore taken over from the pursuit and practice of religion, which used to be respectable, but is no longer, at least in the west. 'For everything its season,' was the unknown Hebrew preacher's conclusion, 'and for every activity under heaven its time,' and a later generation would now want to add Religion – all religions – to that list.

Religion has been weighed in the scales by a general public that no longer defers to handed down practices and beliefs, and has been found to be wanting. Religion has been labelled controlling and a contributor to war. It matters little that research has shown that of the thirty-two wars of the twentieth century, only three had any significant religious element, the rest having either a minimal element or absolutely none at all. Current thinking dictates that perception is everything, and the perception is that religion is bad, spirituality is good.

Gone are the days when the ancient universities of Oxford and Cambridge could describe Divinity as the Queen of Sciences because of its claim to integrate otherwise disconnected disciplines, and undergraduates be seen hastening down narrow cobbled lanes between gleaming spires, to be regaled by venerable dons on St Augustine's proofs for the existence of God. The mental framework that enabled scholars and commoners alike to take on board as reasonable and sound, arguments from contingency, no longer exists: that something is true by virtue of the way things are, rather than by logical necessity. In their often cold and draughty lecture rooms the young would find their convictions reinforced, not undermined, by arguments for the existence of God from the order and beauty of the world, from the eternal principles of human reason and the moral arguments from conscience.

In their college chapels and without irony they could add their voices to that of the psalmist, that it is only 'reckless hearts' who say that 'there is no God'; and until recently few would probably dissent. The expression captures the certainty, not only of a Biblical world, but well beyond it, up to the Renaissance. However pluralistic or monotheistic, crude or refined, for the majority of the inhabitants of the globe, God was a given. Arguments from contingency and the like however no longer ring bells for those outside any of the great religious systems. Darwin has unlocked for us the secrets of the origin of species, and Freud the ego that was once our soul. Marx has described religion as the 'opium of the people'. Even among those who are religious, but approach their faith from a liberal rather than a fundamentalist stance, the concept of God becomes harder to explain. Many genuinely thoughtful and caring people remain to be convinced.

Moreover there is a widespread tendency now to see religion – 'belief in and worship of a super-human controlling power, especially a personal God or gods' - and of sects within the same religion as much as between religions, as the cause of much of the modern world's unrest, whether that divinity is called Jehovah, Our Father in Heaven, Allah, or Vishnu's Thousand names of God. The general public has also shown itself loathe to support charities with a religious ethos, relegating one aid agency, with an avowedly Christian approach, to the category of 'least regarded', according to the findings of one British poll. The decline in church attendance in the traditional strongholds of the Christian faith, certainly in Europe, and more recently in the United States, attest to the same turning away from religion, at least in its denominational brandings.

Yet, alongside extensive disillusionment with various religious packages, some with impeccable pedigrees, other surveys indicate that the concept of 'the other' (which is the heart of religion) continues to engage and enthral the attention of large majorities of the population. The first United Kingdom census of the twenty first century revealed that over seventy-five per cent of people who answered the question about religion said they belonged to a particular religious tradition. Admittedly, for many that may have been no more than a cultural label – such and such a religion is part of my identity, has contributed to making me the person I am, and accounts for the values of the society I subscribe to.

Nevertheless, for many it will also have been a faith statement. A belief that there is more to life than mere existence, and that there is, or at least may be, something 'other' or beyond with which they can and sometimes do interact, some life force with whom they can connect, however sporadically and imperfectly, that can make a difference in terms of personal development and social cohesion. It is as if, in wanting to distance themselves from religion, which they see as preoccupied with systems and dogma, many now find themselves more comfortable with the concept of spirituality, with its emphasis on direct, individual experience.

Spirituality is no longer the arcane interest of the eccentric of extremist. It is a respectable subject for academic study as well as of individual pursuit. It is now possible to do research degrees in spirituality and to attend residential conferences in well appointed centres set in rolling countryside to explore and to discover more about what's involved. It is one of those tides that 'taken at its flood' may not lead to fortune, but that does allow many to find personal fulfilment and satisfaction in a non-religious way. Significantly, according to the director of a British and Irish spirituality network, in contrast to the falling away in church attendance, 'there is no such exodus from our Cathedrals, or from many religious retreat houses. Quite the opposite, because these are the places where people, whether religiously inclined or un-churched, can still encounter the numinous, the sacred, silence, and mystery: the space to be themselves and live their questions.'

Is spirituality, though, not just another name for religion? Aren't we playing with semantics here like some illusionist who by sleight of hand persuades us that now we see it, now we don't? Is the whole spirituality bandwagon not a very clever piece of re-branding in which the word 'religion' has got dumped, but the substance kept? The fundamentals haven't changed but it's had a bit of a make-over. It's the same content, but the bottle's a different shape; only the packaging is new? Can spirituality not become too easily a retreat from the reality that religion can't avoid, and has to face, often with painful consequences?

It is the retreat from reality that underlies the story of Brân, king of the Isle of the Mighty, in one of the great Mediaeval Celtic tales, The Mabinogion. The seven survivors of a campaign to rescue Brân's sister, the beautiful Branwen, from a life of humiliation in the Irish court, find sanctuary on a little island close to home. There, with nothing other than the head of Brân their dead leader for a talisman, they pass the next eighty years in a state of collective amnesia. In the safety of their island retreat, sheltered from the prevailing south westerly winds, with puffins and gannets for company, they have no recollection of the angst that brought Branwen to an early grave, or of the cause of her humiliation, or of the losses sustained to bring her home. All they can remember are Brân's solemn words that they are not to open the third door of their royal refuge. 'As soon as you open that door,' he had warned, 'you can stay no longer.' Spirituality can and does have a similar appeal, a state of being that's apart, a place of safety in uncertain times, an idyllic haven, away from and above the pains and uncertainties of everyday living.

There are clearly different reasons for the current success of spirituality in making faith, as it were, politically correct, that it's OK not to go to the church, gurdwara, mosque, synagogue, or temple, and to have no more than a passing knowledge of their holy books, and of the stories behind their beliefs, and still to consider yourself, and be considered by others, a person of faith, and indeed to follow some kind of devotional practice, either alone or in company. For those who have rejected or have become indifferent to religion, part of the appeal of spirituality is that it offers an alternative way-in to faith. It confirms the conviction that there's more to life than eating, drinking, having sex, playing, sleeping, that there's more to me than the sum total of these activities. But it does so without the prohibitions, without the 'Thou shalt nots'. For those who have rejected religion outright, spirituality still offers points of contact that allow both to walk together for as much of the way as they can; to hear, what Einstein called 'the music of the spheres'.

At the heart of such music, however careful and cautious they may be in accounting for it in terms of a developed theology of divinity, many who have closed the door on religion will still be wanting to keep the door open to spirituality. They will be reluctant to rule out the possibility of being connected in some perhaps indefinable way to something greater than themselves; someone who is wholly beyond but who has the attributes to care, to love and to be loved, ceaselessly reaching out for them like some unrequited lover. In his most famous poem, 'The Hound of Heaven', Francis Thompson describes the sensation as one of being pursued by God:

'Fear wist not to evade as Love wist to pursue.
Still with unhurrying chase and unperturbed pace
Deliberate speed, majestic instancy,
Came on the following feet, and a Voice above their beat:
Nought shelters thee who wilt not shelter Me.'

A century later in R S Thomas's poetry, the reverse is the case. For Thomas, it is we who pursue God; and it's a very elusive God who at best can only be discerned in passing, and the priest struggling in prayer on his knees remembers that:

'peering once
through my locked fingers
I thought that I detected
the movement of a curtain'.

Thomas' is a God who plays hide and seek with us endlessly as if God enjoys the game but never wants to be found, whereas the opposite is true in Thompson's poem. His God is very much out in the open, and if it too is a game of hide and seek, it is humanity that is hiding and not wanting to be found, or at least pretending as much. The truth maybe lies somewhere in between. 'A sight of his love is the cause of our love; and our thirst after him is but the effect of his thirst after us,' wrote another, earlier poet, William Williams of Pantycelyn; 'and our diligence in seeking after him is the effect of his diligence in seeking of us.' As in most human relationships, the initiative will be constantly shifting backwards and forwards in line with the insights of psychology that relationships only stay together and grow where there is a constant moving to and fro, the one pulling the other forward at one time, the other at another.

Much has been made of the final words of the passengers on the ill fated flight 175 on its suicidal path into one of the World Trade Centre's twin towers in New York on the 11th September 2001, that realising they had only moments to live before they were to perish, the last messages sent from mobile phones were not: 'Why me, God?' or 'Why is this happening to me?' but 'I love you.' The wisdom literature of the Hebrews in extolling human love in all its erotic and altruistic potential confirms the belief that it is love that is also the clue to understanding the potential of the human-divine relationship. 'I sleep, but my heart is awake. Listen! My beloved is knocking', says the mortal bride. And the divine groom replies, 'Many waters cannot quench love, no flood can sweep it away; if someone were to offer for love all the wealth in his house, it would be laughed to scorn.' Love is spirituality's inner strength.

At a meeting to run a church in England's home counties, its members were startled into a new awareness of the inclusivity of God's love when Ken, a distinguished religious educator and a chief examiner in religious studies, who already had two major books on religious learning under his belt, led them in prayer. His words had clearly spoken to their hearts and challenged their minds, but before the chair was able to thank him for his thoughtful devotions, Ken announced that the first had been from a Christian source, the second Buddhist and the third Red Indian! That was some years back and they were a reasonably liberal bunch. Even so it had been pretty daring. Since then, that kind of appropriation has become more common, and if we like a prayer or a poem, and it speaks to our condition, we absorb it regardless and without the slightest feeling of guilt. And that is surely right. A faith that does not grow atrophies. The wider our circle of friends, the more rounded a person we become, and that is part of the appeal of spirituality. It gives permission to select because love cannot be constrained.

Selection though needs to be balanced if its fruit is to have lasting worth. The Russian cellist, Mstislav Rostropovich, was not only one of the greatest exponents of his instrument, he was also a person of immense humanity and integrity. Interviewed ahead of a concert he was to give in Paris, his questioner asked whether he had any regrets about the way his life had turned out. 'I tell you now,' replied the maestro, 'if God ask me after I died, you would like I give you another time on earth, you would like something changed? I reply no, I would like repeat my life from beginning to end.' And did that include, his interviewer pressed him, his support for the proscribed author Alexander Solzhenitsyn, which had led to Rostropovich being stripped of his Russian citizenship and expelled from the Soviet Union in 1974? 'Yes, yes,' said the great man, 'because if you not coming to big tragedy, you do not understand what is big joy. It must be like that for performer – if you not play pianissimo, you not understand fortissimo.' Spirituality's attraction is that it allows one to take the best from the faith experiences of the world's religions, but it will not tide one over life's rougher seas, unless there's pianissimo as well as fortissimo in it.

Too often religion has been presented in such a way as to nurture a kind of permanent parent-child mentality, where regardless that we've grown up in every other way, we have been left to see God, through the spiritual aspect of our being, as an indulgent or even capricious elder. Jim was a faithful member of his Midlands church. A widower, he nevertheless always showed a cheerful exterior. One day he confided in his minister that every night before he went to sleep, he knelt by his bed to say a prayer. And what was that prayer? Charles Wesley's children's hymn:

'Gentle Jesus, meek and mild,
Look upon a little child,
Pity my simplicity,
Suffer me to come to Thee'.

What, his pastor asked himself as he made his weary way back to his study, had happened, that this good man whom he'd grown to like and respect, who was more than twice his age, should still be seeing his relationship with God in such simplistic and inadequate terms? Why had we allowed him to be denied the interpretation of a faith that could play 'pianissimo'?

Four men once strode out of the town where they lived and worked, to climb a nearby mountain. We don't know what they looked like, whether they were short or tall, slight or well built, but we know they were young and that they were serious about what they were about. Two were brothers, quite a fiery pair - James and John. With their friend, Peter, the three of them formed quite a close knit bunch. The other one, Jesus, was a bit of an enigma. How much of an enigma, they were soon to find out. Bit by bit they left behind the everyday sounds of the market and the home, of the workplace and the street; the voices of their companions, the squealing of their children, of business orders being taken and despatched, of priests rustling their way to their temple duties, and rabbis reciting from well used scrolls, of the steel clash of Roman swords scraping the ground, and the inane babble of the sane and the insane.

Up they went, their ears becoming attuned to the rustlings in the undergrowth as chameleons and lizards scurried out of their way or they disturbed a snake slithering noiselessly over the hot earth as it sloughed off its outgrown skin like a past life. Up they went, missing their footing here and there, dislodging the odd stone, their weathered calves scratched by the occasional thorn or the spines of a cactus, swigging a mouthful of water now and again from their leather carriers and chewing on bits of dry bread. And the higher they climbed the greater their sense of seeing things differently, of looking back over the way they'd come, and realising the smallness of all they'd left behind, almost its irrelevance in the perspective of the peaks. The air they breathed smelt fresher, cooler, though their exertions still made them sweat.

Along the way they stopped to pray. Sometimes in the shade of a crag. Sometimes under the unremitting sun. Sometimes on their knees. Sometimes, like the prophets of old, standing upright with arms outstretched and the wind ruffling their hair, to do business with God, face to face. Sometimes in low voices carried away on the wind. Sometimes loud and argumentative, disputing and putting their human case with Torah and Mishnah, chapter and verse, for evidence. And always waiting for a response. For confirmation that they'd been heard. Some indication inside that the conversation had not been one way.

Stopping and starting. Sometimes exchanging thoughts, a memory or a joke with each other, but most of the time silently to save their breath for the higher reaches. And somewhere along the way they met Moses and Elijah, and they heard the voice of God. At least that was how they described it later to the others, who'd been left behind, below, resentful at having been made to miss out. In the same poem in which R S Thomas wrote of the 'movement of a curtain' he described:

'Prayers like gravel
flung at the sky's
window, hoping to attract
the loved one's
attention'

This was such a moment for them. Just for a second perhaps, or longer, they saw things differently, they saw Jesus in a fresh light, transfigured, like coming on a familiar face or figure from an unexpected angle. Trying to explain it afterwards it fell flat, it failed to convince, because the others weren't there, they didn't see it as they saw it. Maybe the others didn't want to. Maybe they resented being expected to appreciate an experience second hand. Because it must have been irritating if not hurtful to be one of the nine left behind. It would have been surprising if they hadn't talked among themselves, questioning why Peter, James and John had been favoured, and not for the first time either? But questioning more the motives of Jesus. He had come across as someone with a fresh vision of God. Who took on the religious establishment of his day with its hierarchy of access to the divine presence: its outer court, its inner court, and its holy of holies, and he had preached a message of spiritual equality.

How too did Peter, James and John feel about being chosen? Did they feel embarrassed or were they so absorbed in their own little world, and excited at what Jesus would share with them and reveal to them on this rather intimate expedition, that they never considered its effect on the rest of the group. Religion, even at its most refined, can still be a very divisive influence, even among its own committed adherents. At the time though they'd seen Jesus in the light of eternity, and it was a moment they'd wanted to capture forever. They had touched holy ground, and they wished for it never to end. Like the heroes of the Celtic myth they too wanted to build a refuge for themselves above the sea and to dwell there endlessly with their beloved leader. But he had other ideas for them and for those left behind. Realistic spirituality needed to touch base.

2. A worse mess:
spirituality as religion's inspiration

'I remember, I remember
The house where I was born'

As dawn bleached the Southern Cross out of the indigo sky above Canberra, and they made their silent, sleepy way to the big tent on the city's outskirts, they were not to know how continuity would be made to creep into the crevices of their imagination that morning and into the secret places of their personal histories. They came from the five continents in their bright saris, dresses, skirts, casual tee shirts, frayed denims, pink and black cassocks, to worship at the beginning of day; fifteen hundred of them. And as they filed in through the mammoth marquee's open flaps they were handed squares of coloured fabric no bigger than an envelope. To the primitive throb of the didgeridoo and the clipped notes of the guitar, the beat of the drum and the clicking of clap-sticks, they sang their hymns in Spanish and German, French and English, and listened again to the old, old story of their faith in a clutch of minority languages.

Then someone told them to write on their little squares of cloth, to inscribe a name of someone who had brought them to that place in the southern hemisphere that February morning. Mother, father, daughter, son; sister, brother; grandparent, friend; teacher, pastor, priest; someone who'd touched their lives with the flame of faith and had awakened an awareness of God in them. Later their ragged bits of material would be threaded together and hung in a long loop around the canvas walls, a vivid, personal pattern proclaiming that, regardless of tongue or colour, they were there, each and every one of them, because someone, somewhere had taken the trouble to pass on the story

23

it come alive for them. Because spirituality that fails to recognise its roots in the flesh and blood reality of religion is too vague to have anything meaningful or lasting to offer the flesh and blood pilgrim.

Russell T Davies, one of television's most innovative writers, who says he spent his childhood avoiding Welsh Sunday Schools, and is now more comfortable describing himself as an atheist, nevertheless expresses concern at what has replaced religion for many people. 'We are living in a very cynical age where religion is laughed at,' he admits, 'and yet where a lot of us have our own hotchpotch of weird beliefs and Do It Yourself creeds.' Though spirituality and religion may appear to be at odds with each other, and many may be glad to embrace the one and to do so quite openly while being wary or even antipathetic to the other, if spirituality is to flourish it will need the memory, the discernment and the social critique of religion.

For those for whom spirituality offers a way out of the negative underworld of religion into the light and liberation of a freethinking faith, such a proposition may be distasteful or even preposterous. But spirituality didn't fall ready made out of the sky one spring morning. Each and every religion's spirituality grew out of a tradition, a particular tradition, and cannot be understood apart from that tradition. That's its genealogy. And unless it keeps faith with that genealogy it will career off on its own orbit, as some spiritualities have already done, lost in an outer space which is inaccessible and irrelevant. As individuals, we understand ourselves better as we discover more about those who make up our particular lineage. My family tree has thrown up what appears at first sight to be a random mix of occupations common to the period, the culture, the location and the class to which my antecedents belonged. And of course their choices will have been as broad and as narrow as the expectations of their place in the social order of their age.

But that is only a partial and a superficial picture. What the birth, marriage and death certificates fail to record or the parish registers and census results to reveal are the character traits, the strengths and weaknesses of this mixed bunch whose DNA I've inherited. There are few surviving letters to flesh out the bare details, and the sepia portraits with their fixed smiles or sober stares give few clues into the inner lives of their subjects. What made them tick? What pushed some of them forwards to take up positions of modest leadership in their communities, while others were less forthcoming?

The answers to such questions are lost now and a matter of guesswork, but certain common traits colour my particular tree. There are quite strong Presbyterian and Baptist threads running through my tribe. Faith was a serious issue for them, not just a cultural badge. I see some too who prided themselves in their work: craftsmen in wood and stone, a self taught architect, men for whom detail mattered and shoddy work was unacceptable. I see creative types, too: the pianist who was a child prodigy and composed Schubertian songs; and an idealist who taught himself Esperanto: the invented language that was supposed to increase universal co-operation but never really caught on. And some of the women had strong characters and clear minds, and conducted themselves, raised their families and ran their homes with the same seriousness with which they sang the hymns of Ann Griffiths and Pantycelyn on a Sunday. Because it was all of a piece.

Each spirituality similarly has its distinctive tree. The spirituality being embraced may appear to have broken away or even to be a new species, but its DNA will uncover a basic inherited structure that reveals its religious origins. To neglect those origins is to become disconnected from a past that explains and accounts for the shape and feel of what and how we believe now. The Hebrew child is taught from an early age to remember the rock from which his people were hewn. At the annual Passover meal, the next generation is instructed in the story of his people: 'My father was a homeless Aramaean who went down to Egypt and lived there with a small band of people, but there it became a great, powerful, and large nation.'

At the annual festival of Baisakhi, the Sikh boy and girl hear again how their people trace their origins to the Khalsa, the initiation of the five 'pure ones' as a brotherhood: 'There is one God; His name is truth, The all pervading Creator, Without fear, without hatred; Immortal, unborn, self existent.' The Hindu youth's rite of passage is marked by the Upanayana, during which he is taught the secret of life and receives a sacred thread to wear until he dies. The young Moslem is brought up to know the Hadith literature which concentrates on the life and sayings of Muhammad so that the Muslim can live in a manner worthy of this great prophet. Many Buddhists undergo a ceremony in which they emulate the life of Buddha in leaving their father and mother and travelling to the monastery for a time of asceticism and meditation. And in certain Theravada traditions key events from the life of the Buddha are displayed in these monasteries. And in the practice of the Eucharist or Holy Communion children in the Christian family remember 'that on a certain night its Founder said and did certain definite things, briefly reported .... The remembrance goes back in a continuous chain .... For nineteen centuries there has not been one single week in which this act of remembrance was not made, one generation reminding another.' Without continuity we are lost in an aimless present. Remembering his childhood home, the house where he was born, and the loss of innocence that comes with age, Thomas Hood can only grieve that:

'... now tis little joy
To know I'm farther off from heav'n
Than when I was a boy'

Remembering matters if we are to understand the whys and

wherefores of where we now are. It was high up on the slopes above the garrison town of Caesarea Philippi that Simon Peter and his companions made the connection between Jesus, who had brought a new spirituality into their lives, and the Judaism in which he and they had been grounded and which still shaped their existence. For Peter, impetuous, but intuitive, it proved a decisive turning point. He'd a wife back home, children and an ailing mother in law to support. Yet here he was, having hitched his wagon to this new phenomenon from Nazareth, Galilee's one donkey town. Thanks to brothers, cousins, stay at home friends he managed to keep the family solvent and fed with a bit of fishing by night and in-between the tours. But there was a lot of criticism that he'd walked out on his responsibilities.

Peter, wanting, trying to be responsible, vying with Peter the taker of risks, on a mountain like Sinai where Moses had once heard the voice of God in a cloud, the 'I am that I am', and come away from the encounter with a radiance that dazzled. Conservative Peter, rigid about keeping the law and the practices of his people because that was what it was to be Jewish, to belong to a chosen people, in an inner turmoil over whether Jesus, charismatic rabbi that he was, was kosher. And there it was, being played out before his very eyes, and in his head, there on the mountain side. Moses had joined them! Moses, magnificent, majestic, magisterial, and as craggy as Michelangelo would one day carve him out of a marble block. The law giver himself, their founding father as the people of the Torah, standing beside Jesus and endorsing him. And 'I am that I am', again speaking from a cloud, and Jesus radiant. Jesus, rooted in the tradition of Moses, but going beyond it without losing it.

Mountains had always played a significant part in their history. But this mountain was like no other. Afterwards people would point to Tabor, Jezreel's sugarloaf, or to snow capped Hermon, as the site of where it had happened. But for those who'd been there with Jesus it could have been anywhere and for ever after was everywhere. Roots matter, and the roots of spirituality are the religion from which it has sprung. Spirituality is too important to be allowed to fray at the edges because it has begun to lose its memory. Without roots, spirituality can quickly become meaningless. Their experience on the mountain wasn't an introduction to an alternative religion. It was rooted in the religious tradition and history of their people.

On their way up Jesus had told them a story. 'Once a dirty old tramp was thrown out of an empty house where he had been squatting.' They knew of plenty like that. 'He looked all round the town for somewhere suitable to sleep but couldn't find anywhere. Then he thought he would try his old place again.' Their eyes showed surprise. 'It was still empty so he broke in. He saw someone had cleaned up his mess while he had been away. Then he had an idea.' Their curiosity well roused, Jesus continued, 'He invited seven other tramps even more dirty than himself to share the squat. The mess they all made together was much worse than when he had lived there on his own' (Good as New translation). They laughed at lot at that, but they never forgot it. It is the story of the iconoclast; the fanatic in every age who, in the pursuit of a purer version of the tradition, and its application, destroys without replacing; who rejects religion because of its imperfections and is surprised to find as a consequence that spirituality has become chaotic and destructive.

Ed Husain was brought up as part of a devout Muslim family in East London. It was a tolerant, interfaith world where his and his family's friends were Christian, Hindu, Sikh and Jew as well as Muslim. A bright boy, adolescence became a nightmare in a low achieving single sex secondary school where he became introverted and withdrawn. Increasingly alienated from mainstream British society, at first he found the message of the extremists who preached that 'All others, including fellow Muslims, were wrong and heading for hell' very enticing. His account of how he became progressively involved with those he dubs the 'Islamists' before realising the inherent dangers of extremism makes fascinating if controversial reading. 'Beware of extremism in religion,' he quotes from the Prophet Muhammad, 'for it was extremism in religion that destroyed those who went before you.' The youngsters from Seventh Day Adventist homes who joined David Koresh's Branch Davidians at Waco in Texas, and died in the inferno when the police moved in, were similarly attracted by someone offering a purer more extreme spirituality than anything they'd experienced before. The Jim Jones cult in Guiana tells a similar story. And every world religion will have its own roll call of those who have been deceived in their quest for the spirituality they sought. These extreme cults may masquerade as religion, but are in effect expressions of a fanatical spirituality, where, in offering to expel the demons of alienation and low self esteem, they have invaded the sacred space at the heart of every individual with a frightening gaggle of sinister and destructive forces.

The expelling of one squatter only to be invaded by a plague of worse squatters is also something that society, not just religion, needs to address. Society has to understand why so many young people are susceptible to 'dark spirituality' – the spirituality that fuels civil unrest, violence and terrorism. It was because of his work over a lifetime of arguing that society must take spirituality far more seriously than it does that Charles Taylor, a professor of political science at McGill University, Montreal, was awarded the 2007 Templeton prize, for 'progress toward research or discoveries about spiritual realities'. Society has to realise, he argued, that socio-economic reasons alone do not provide the answer as to why this extreme form of spirituality is so attractive to those who otherwise see their lives as meaningless, rootless and purposeless.

It is an illusion of secular western democracies that improving its citizens' material situation will automatically and alone lead to a more stable society and to happier people. No government can satisfy its people's spiritual needs and aspirations, and it is dangerous if any try, but they can provide a culture in which the hunger for meaning is not seen as an aberration or a regrettable sign of arrested growth on the part of its citizens. They can affirm the value of discernment in matters of religion as in every other sphere of our life together. In creating a secular society, with all the freedoms and plurality which that entails, we have lost the values that a proper recognition of religion, of its place and purpose, provide. People are looking for spiritual direction to their lives, and if they do not find it in good religion they will find it in bad, because as individuals and communities we need that sense of purpose to our lives which religion provides: to see our lives in terms of the meta narrative; to see where and how we fit into the larger picture of who we are, why we're here and what we're for.

As our culture has privatised religion, it has discovered that the social cohesion religion once provided has been lost, and is paying a high price for it. Spirituality needs religion. But, so does society, because without God, what has Moses to offer? For all their spirituality on the mountain side, Jesus still took Peter, James and John back to synagogue and temple. He endorsed the significance of religion in the nurture and development of spirituality because it provided the memory that spirituality needs if it is to know its antecedents and why it is the way it is.

In the old Celtic tale, as our seven champions came and went through the magnificent entrances of the palace on their island retreat, with chamberlains and young lads to remove their boots and knights to take their armour and dress them in garments of gold and brocaded silk, they were unaware of the price they'd paid for that respite. And it would take very many more years before one of them had the courage to face up to what was happening to them and to do something about it. What was it that had happened back in the Isle of the Mighty over which Brân had ruled that was too awful to recall? What memories were locked in their subconscious, that made them toss and turn at night and to cry out in their sleep so that the guards came running? And what was the sadness that brooded over their company even when they ate and caroused to their heart's content?

In reminding spirituality of the roots from which it sprung, religion has that more sombre role: to act as a reminder of a troubled past it might wish to forget but needs to hold onto if it is to keep faith with reality. Because religion's most necessary contribution to faith is to help it to be honest. In every family there will be the story tellers, who, over a pint in the local, or a dreamy moment after a family meal, will fill in the gaps, sometimes leaving the story suspiciously half told, sometimes letting the cat out of the bag, but always reminding us, sometimes uncomfortably, of where we've come from and who we are. As I look back at my family tree I see we too had our share of wild cards; those we didn't refer to or only mentioned in hushed tones: some who drank too much; the lad who joined a paramilitary organisation; those who strayed from their marriage vows, or had babies out of wedlock.

In every religious tradition there will be similar stories that embarrass and many that appal. Things attributed to God, and done in the name of God, that must make God cringe and creation tremble. When we hear this awful record incorporated into a liturgical setting, or read it for ourselves, there is a mounting urge by the liberal believer to excise it from the record permanently, to erase or air brush it out of the history of our religion. Or next best to have it never referred to again, particularly in company, and if possible detached from regular worship or, out of respect for the historian, relegated to the archives to gather dust and hopefully be forgotten.

But we cannot afford to forget the awful bits, because it is in remembering them that we realise the incompleteness of our grasp of God over successive generations, and wonder at God's persistent interest in us. Memory is vital, collective, corporate and individual. It provides us with our identity because continuity demands that we recall the feuds as well as the friendships, the hurts as well as the loves. Continuity requires us to learn from the past, to accept our place in the ongoing life that is our tribe, but not to be trapped by it. There are memories to be savoured. There are others to be healed. The danger with a spirituality that sees itself as different from, or replacing rather than enhancing and contributing to religion is that it implies that faith is the prerogative of a personal experience of God that is separated from the mess of life as it is, mine and other people's.

The encouragement of religion on the other hand is that it does not offer an alternative, other worldly answer to life, but a way of living that may rarely if ever reach the heights proclaimed from its pulpits and celebrated on its altars but that saves us from the despair of thinking and believing that this is the best we can ever expect to be. The twentieth century has been called the worst in the history of human kind because of the cruelties we unleashed on each other. And in the sober roll call of those times, the most defining for many will be the dropping of history's first atom bomb on Hiroshima. By some strange irony that sheds an uncomfortable light on our spiritual shortcomings the 6th of August, the day the Enola Gay released its terrible payload, was also the date earmarked in the Christian calendar for commemorating that other moment on a mountain side in a land far away and long ago, when the flash of light was Divine and the cloud a canopy of kindness.

Today's Hiroshima has grown up on the edge of the city that used to exist before bring reduced to a crater. The one busy and bustling, the other interred and still, a park promoting peace with a bell to peal, with a green hill respectfully marked off behind railings to cover the bones and the ashes of those who had perished. On school days children on educational outings come to drape funeral streamers on the memorials, and to sing in harmony for the long dead and the now living. To hear again of Sadako

Sasaki who'd once been their age, but had died of the effects of radiation before she could grow up, but had lived long enough to fold thousands of paper cranes, whispering over each one, 'I will write peace on your wings, and you will fly all over the world.'

Across the river the shell of a building that survived total obliteration hovers heavily on its buckled frame. And in the museum among the other grotesque exhibits and life size models, those stone steps that had once ushered the shoes of its hurrying customers into and out of the bank but that now bear forever the negative of a single, solitary human shadow permanently imprinted by a man-made sun that fell from the sky one clear summer morning.

Keiji Nakazawa was seven when it happened. His cartoon book, Barefoot Gen, which is largely autobiographical, has been translated into many languages and is still read. Gen's father had been against the war, and he and his family had been ostracised as unpatriotic. But there were no patriots or pacifists on 6th of August 1945, just victims. 'Wheat pushes its shoots up through the winter frost,' Gen meditates, 'only to be stepped on again and again.'

'My God, what have we done?' the chaplain who blessed the plane that carried the bomb asked himself afterwards. Because we were all complicit, whatever the strategic arguments for and against, whatever side we were on, whatever our racial identity. Religion is not a get out, but a carefully choreographed litany to help us face up to reality, with an implicit promise that in our worst acts, our worst moments, we are not beyond redemption.

As the southern cross was lost in the brightness of a new day, the successors of those events nearly half a century earlier knelt alongside each other in the unity of their religion as did the successors of the world's other conflicts. As the languages of the nations were translated into the silence of worship they saw Jesus again keeping company with Moses and Elijah, though this time as fallible human beings needing healing for their own memories.

And those who heard the voice of God that day heard it because they recognised their past. And what they heard would shape their future.

When Shelagh Stephenson called her successful West End play about family ties 'The Memory of Water' she was inviting the audience to see how similar homeopathy and heredity are. Because no matter how far one dilutes the original substance, it's always there. In the play, three sisters, Teresa, Mary and Catherine are brought together to arrange their mother's funeral, and in the process have to deal with the fall out of their shared but differently remembered family history.

For many in the developed world the memory of religion is now quite faint. That it persists nevertheless is an indication not only that most of us cannot understand our history without it, but that we still believe that all is not lost. Without religion what spirituality has to offer can be shallow and superficial. But that is still only half the story.

3. Outside both worlds:
religion as spirituality's memory

'... something religious in the way we sit
At the tea table'

The hall off platform two of the Sirkeci train station in Istanbul was almost full when we arrived. The delicate pink and blue of the Moorish tracery on its ornate ceiling had once looked down on the titled and affluent of Europe and the world as they waited impatiently to board the Orient Express for Venice. Today it surveyed an audience of casually dressed tourists seated on three sides of its lofty honey-pale walls in excited talkative anticipation. We had come to witness a performance of mystic music and dance by the Sufi group of the Galata Mevlevi Lodge.

What were we expecting? Three hundred of us: children and grownups, teenagers and seniors, with our electronic cameras, worn haversacks and bulging shoulder bags. Certainly something spectacular, out of the ordinary, perhaps even exotic. Few anticipated a spiritual experience. But that's what we got. As the early evening light filtered sympathetically through the speckled rose window high above our heads a dozen black cloaked Sufis, women and men, in tall slender hats – some white, some the colour of the soil, quietly took their places along the fourth wall. Flautists and drummers, chanters and choir stilled our chatter and heightened our awareness as they wooed us with their music; gradually, mystically transforming that impersonal space in that unlikely location near the waterfront, where ferries docked and cargo was loaded, into a chamber fit for The Sema, the famous Whirling Ceremony.

Then they began to spin. They made obeisance, threw off their long black cloaks, and with arms that had previously been folded across their chests, raised one to point to heaven and lowered the other to point to the earth. Then with eyes closed they began circling the floor, their full-skirted long white gowns fanning out around them. This was no longer a performance. These were not entertainers. These were devotees sharing with us a unique spiritual journey from the self to the divine: life-like tops in ivory and bronze, spinning, spinning to the glory of God, impervious to interruptions from passenger noise on the platform outside, or time-table information from a distorting tannoy.

This was a dance of love. These were lovers, momentarily losing themselves in the divine love so that they could return to their everyday world of commerce and trade, study and care to live better, more thoughtful, more considerate lives. And as we watched them we too were drawn into their ecstatic absorption in God. As they whirled and span, as they revolved and twirled, ever faster, giddyingly faster, breathtakingly, ethereally agile, our spirits rose with theirs and for a moment we too had that sense of being completely at one, with the universe, with our fellow human beings, with God himself. We were witnessing an ecstatic flight into the infinite. We were, consciously or unconsciously, worshipping God, a God whose nature was love, unconditional, universal, eternal love. And it ennobled us.

As we left that railway station built for a bygone age beneath the stout walls of the Topkapi Palace, where sultans had once ruled an empire and controlled a caliphate, where women had been hidden and harems regulated, to board our trams for journeys to cafes, hotels, apartments and houses, we were just that bit different. Whether many would have put it into so many words, or even acknowledged the spirituality of the experience, we had worshipped.

Sufism is the Moslem spirituality. There may be some in Islam who find that its emphasis on the individual's absorption on God sits uneasily with the practical teaching of the Qur'an, but it is not to the exclusion of all else but in order to become more integrated with life. And since the mystic poet, Jalal al-Din Rumi, first nurtured it eight hundred years ago it has drawn adherents from across the Islamic world. 'Choose love that you might be a chosen one,' Rumi proclaimed. 'Be like me and know; whether in light or darkness, until you have been like this you can't completely know love. Be a lover, a lover. Choose love that you might be a chosen one.'

It was an Armenian Christian who introduced me to Sufism. I was struggling to find the point of contact between Christianity with its emphasis on the love of God and Islam with its emphasis on the mercy of God. As I picked at my mezzehs late at night in one of Aleppo's up-market restaurants, my Syrian host showed me how Christian and Moslem can not only live at peace with each other, but in a shared spirituality. 'If you enter the Sema you will leave both worlds:' of the self and of its surroundings, Rumi prophesied; 'the world of the Sema is outside both worlds.'

Spirituality needs religion if it is not to lose its sense of continuity with the tradition which gave it birth, and nurtured it. However uneasily it may sit alongside religion, it cannot ignore or dismiss it lightly. It's where it's come from, and if it is to continue to have something to say and not to moulder into a miasma of vague sentiments and muddled thought, it will need to acknowledge and to hold fast to its religious roots.

But equally religion needs spirituality if its practices and dogmas, if its hierarchies and liturgies are to speak to the heart as well as the head. Nature may require procreation for the survival of the human species, but it is 'falling in love' that makes it more than a mechanistic response to a biological instinct. Chemistry alone does not account for a brilliant mediaeval scholar like Peter Abelard reflecting on his passion for Heloise, 'I conducted my classes in a mood of lukewarm indifference. I no longer spoke from inspiration, but from memory. I did little more than repeat my earlier lessons, and if I felt free enough in my mind to compose a few scraps of verse it was love and not philosophy which dictated them to me.'

Nor will social convention alone explain the feelings behind the stylised Taoist etiquette of a letter from the young wife of the sixteenth century Japanese aristocrat to her husband, the Lord Kumura Shigenari, governor of Nagato. Should he die in battle thus denying them the happiness of growing old together she will kill herself, she tells him. 'I know that when two wayfarers "take shelter under the same tree and slake their thirst in the same river" it has all been determined by their karma from a previous life. ... I shall be waiting for you at the end of what they call the road to death.'

Or of Pierre Curie's letter to his future wife Marie: 'It would be a fine thing ... in which I hardly dare believe, to pass our lives near each other, hypnotised by our dreams: your patriotic dream, our humanitarian dream, and our scientific dream.' Nor can we dismiss the love poetry of the centuries as no more than beautiful but empty literary indulgences: a Shakespeare's 'Shall I compare thee to a summer's day', or a Yeats's 'When you are old and grey and full of sleep', or an Auden's 'stop all the clocks, cut off the telephone'.

In a similar way spirituality can be described as religion's heart. Not simply in terms of its emotional content, though that is important, but also as that which reveals its inner core, its eternal flame. It relates to the non-rational element that makes up the human psyche. Post enlightenment, certainly in the developed world, we still seem to be in thrall to the idea that what cannot be verified by observation and experience is suspect, that reason and individualism are all important. But to be non-rational is not to be irrational. To be non-rational is to acknowledge that there are aspects of our make-up that are not explained in terms of reason and deduction. When the rational becomes all there is, we cut ourselves off from tapping into those elements of our existence that ultimately give life its meaning.

Though religion by definition has to do with the non-rational, in practice it can appear, and often is, more mechanistic than mysterious. Hence its need to recognise that spirituality is not an optional extra. It is not just a matter of religion's well being but of its very essence. It may preach peace; it may advocate love; it may demand justice, but unless it can breathe life into them it will not capture the hearts of its adherents, and may ultimately forfeit its claim to their minds.

As the heroes of the Celtic myth whiled away their days and years on their little island retreat, they cut an unreal picture as they wandered about aimlessly among its barren rocks and bleak crags. Suspended between war and peace, injustice and pardon, hatred and love there would be no relief from the numbness of their half life until they were able to confront their ghosts and to grieve for the pains that had come unbidden to their people and had marked the troubled life of the beautiful Branwen.

For Peter, James and John, however, scrambling about among the rocks above Caesarea Philippi, there had been no similar loss of memory. As geckos' quickstepped aside in the harsh sun, leaving Jesus alone with his thoughts and prayers, they argued, they doubted, they struggled to understand what they'd just witnessed. They remembered how, long before, Moses had brought down from mount Sinai the tablets of stone with their ten commandments as the basis for his people's identity and the guarantor of their continued existence, he too had had a personal experience of God.

He told his brother Aaron later that, while he'd been shepherding his father-in-law's flock on Mount Sinai, he'd seen a bush on fire that never burnt out, and heard the voice of God. 'Take off your sandals, for the place where you are standing is holy ground.' God, mysterious and awesome, but somehow attractive too. Attractive enough to make him want to get closer, to go barefoot in the afterglow of the almighty.

And in all the great faiths, there are similar stories of an intense spiritual experience that results in a changed way of life.

For the Buddha, Prince Siddhatha, enlightenment came as he sat beneath a Bodhi tree. For Nanak, the father of Sikhism, the moment of transformation came as he bathed in the river and felt lifted high into the sky and beyond until he was in the very presence of God.

On a mountainside somewhere beyond the cedars of Lebanon, Peter's blustering, un-thought through, instantaneous reaction to the spirituality they'd experienced was to propose they stayed at that level of spiritual intensity more or less permanently. Thoughts of family and companions had now vanished in the sheer delight of this intense experience.

For John though, who could be as wild as James at times but more incisive than Peter, Moses had appeared there besides Jesus, not only to indicate that Jesus was no Jewish maverick, though that was important enough, but to show that behind the laws of his religion there had been an intense moment of mystery and attraction, an encounter with God. And unless that was acknowledged and nurtured, religion became a dry system of dos and don'ts. Religion without spirituality became a desiccated husk. And the school of theology which was later to trace its origins to John was the one based on an experience of God as love, where spirituality gave religion its appeal.

If many in search of spirituality have turned to crystals, to t'ai chi and tarot, it is because the great religions have failed them by keeping their understanding of the meditative, and their expression of the mysterious hidden. 'The hunger for the mysterious, the spiritual and the arcane which is apparent in many people's lives, is a perpetual witness', according to Professor Densil Morgan, 'to the fact that humankind cannot live by bread alone.'

Moreover, whatever weight one chooses to put on some or on all the six thousand and more firsthand accounts of contemporary religious and spiritual experience collected by Alister Hardy's Religious Research Centre, the impression given is that for very many spirituality is no alien concept, but something almost natural.

In research of a more academic kind, conducted by Gordon Lynch, professor of sociology and religion at Birkbeck college in the University of London, the fifty per cent or more of the adult population of the United Kingdom which admits to being faith sensitive, would re-connect with religion if religion was more prepared to show its passion behind its preaching, and significantly a willingness to re-think the significance of place, because there is now a greater readiness to be surprised by God on non-religious, than on traditionally consecrated, ground.

'Earth's crammed with heaven
And every common bush afire with God,'

wrote Elizabeth Barrett Browning, drawing on the story of Moses and the burning bush,

'But only he who sees, takes off his shoes
The rest sit round it and pluck blackberries'.

The world is littered with the empty shells of places that once had the power to move us to the very depth of our being. Chapels converted into carpet showrooms, restaurants or garages, churches with boarded up windows and deconsecrated, temples and synagogues, where moss gathers and lizards hide. The insights of a living spirituality tell us that however it feels, however it looks, it doesn't matter, because holy ground is wherever we encounter God.

It may be a new trend after generations accustomed to the permanence of a particular place, but its roots can be traced to the experience of those early Hebrews, the central focus of whose worship was originally not a temple, but a tent, not a solid inner sanctum but a mobile ark. Many argued, including their own prophets, that their dependence on God was stronger and more vital when their meeting place with their God was always on the move, and could say: this piece of earth, this layer of soil is sacred for me, for us, now, but it may not be so forever. It has no intrinsic right to claim the allegiance of our devotion because it worked for those who came before us or even for us in the past. Its power lies in its immediacy and its portability. Because this is an age of the transitory and the temporary which can nevertheless be the means by which many discover what is worth keeping as they sort through the clutter of their crowded lives.

For some it will come through the lofty architecture of a magnificent place of worship, for others a nondescript meeting house; for some in a great company of people, for others alone; for some in the throng of a pop concert, for others on a walk in the woods; for some in the ecstasy of watching one's favourite team win, for others sailing solo ahead of a perfect wind; for some in the pursuit of a specific rule of life that could be Orthodox, Ignatian or Benedictine; for some in music that makes the soul soar, for others in the silence of a Quaker gathering; for some in dance and Pentecostal outpouring, for others in sacred music that is measured and timeless; for some in the rhythm and vibration of tabla and harmonium, for others in the resonances of a triple pipe organ.

It came for me one dark December night. I was in my twenties, living in Coventry in digs and sitting in a comfortable armchair in my room listening to Handel's oratorio, Messiah. As the long playing vinyl record spun on its turntable I saw no lights, I had no out of body experience, I heard no voices other than those of the London Philharmonic Choir, but I felt God very close. 'Behold, I tell you a mystery,' the bass voice confided. The tenor proclaimed that 'Every valley shall be exalted', and the choir responded with the Hallelujah chorus. 'King of Kings and Lord of Lords' reverberated around the room, and in my innermost being, in a rising crescendo of praise. And I responded: Yes, yes, God. Incarnation,

Trinity, these were just formulae to explain the inexplicable.

There had been other moments of spiritual intensity before and have been since, but none that seared themselves so deeply into my heart and soul. And when the going has proved difficult, and religion soulless, it is the memory of that experience that sustains the vision. So many today find their spirituality nurtured most meaningfully not in a church or a religious building, but in some secular space that becomes for the time holy ground. And religion needs to welcome that and to affirm it.

For the twentieth century poet, Bobi Jones, it was at tea with his wife and daughter that he came nearest to the experience of Peter, James and John on the mountainside two thousand years ago.

'There is something religious in the way we sit
At the tea table, a tidy family of three.
You, my love, slicing bread and butter, and she,
The red-cheeked tot a smear of blackberry jam, and me.
Set apart for the marvellous doting
Of a world's interchange with each other ... that's tea.
Not proper for us to think of the thing as a sacrament,
And yet all the elements are found to change in our hands.
Because we sit and share them with each other
There's a miracle. There's a binding of unmerited graces
By the cheese, and through the apples and milk is established
A new creation of life, a true presence.
And talking to each other, uttering words over food
Is somehow different from customary chatting.'

Places hallowed by time and usage will still have spiritual significance, whether it's the Golden Temple at Amritsar for the Sikhs or the Ka'aba at Mecca for the Muslims; the sacred Ganges for the Hindus or the Wailing Wall in Jerusalem for the Jews; or the church of the Nativity in Bethlehem for Christians. But religion is

43

being challenged as never before to broaden its definition of what's holy, to become more welcoming to the insights which spirituality offers.

If it was John on the mountainside who saw that spirituality was of the essence of religion, it was Peter who realised that spirituality was also its motivation. Once he'd been jolted out of his reverie of remaining in a more or less permanent state of ecstatic bliss, Peter remembered how his people's prophets from Elijah on, had always emphasised the link between faith and action. They'd taught that spirituality could never be a purely private passion. 'If spirituality is more than an abstract idea, it manifests itself in our human responses to the brokenness of our world,' the American Fransiscan, Joan Puls, reminds us; to 'the threats to our planet home, the crisis points in our own lives, and the pleas and plights of human beings around us.'

Confronted by the burning bush Peter realised that Moses may have covered his face in fear, but he could not cover his soul. To engage with God meant there was no escape from engaging with God's concerns, but not before he'd shown a considerable degree of resistance. Raw, untested Moses, long before his transformation into the solid substance of a founding father, innocently and nervously tending his father in law's flock, tortured by memories of what he'd done in Egypt and why. Moses arguing inside his head with and against God, and not in any recognised place of cultic significance, but out in the open and ordinary magnificence of an unforgiving landscape.

Why pick on me? Moses had asked the angel in the bush. I'm not your man. There are abler, holier people around who would do a much better job for you. Anyway I lack the credibility. I'd never pull it off. I don't have the requisite qualifications for a delicate operation of this sort – parleying with a Pharaoh and fomenting a slave rebellion. In any case, I'm not very good with words! But it was bluster in the face of a divine imperative. He did eventually free the Hebrew slaves and make them into a nation with a law to mould and shape them. But it was that moment when he'd stood barefoot before a burning bush that gave him his moral authority.

All religions advocate peace and justice but it is spirituality that feeds and sustains their commitment. So there have been countless generations of Holy fools whose zeal to right a social wrong has been fuelled by their religious convictions. Fools like William Wilberforce and his associates, Thomas Clarkson, Granville Sharpe, and the emancipated slave, Olaudah Equiano, campaigning to get the United Kingdom parliament to abolish its support of the slave trade.

Fools like the four peace activists, Jim Loney, Harmeet Sooden, Tom Fox and Norman Kember, kidnapped in Baghdad. Tom paid with his life, the other three were released, Kember later baffling a sceptical public with his confession: 'I don't regret what I did, because there's an element in Christianity of being foolish.' Fools like Mahatma Gandhi, the high caste Brahmin with a strong element of spirituality, committed to a lifelong duty to improving the lot of the Dalits and to maintaining peace between Hindu and Moslem, and for which he too paid with his life.

Holy fools all of them, who made the connection between soul and service and in the process challenged their religions to recover the spirituality which lies at their centre. Religion will always have need of spiritualities that can underpin its avowed concern for justice: the radical, third world, liberation spiritualities without which religion can lose its cutting edge.

Without spirituality religion will fail to make its voice heard on behalf of the 2.4 million people, half of them children, who are trafficked every year; to take on the arms and drug smugglers; to refuse to accept that torture is ever permissible; to speak up on behalf of the disappeared in every nation; to advocate justice in international trade; to challenge the international community to intervene in areas where genocide is being committed and wars are making millions of people into refugees; to work to eliminate starvation and improve health care among the poorest on earth.

It is sad to see religion often wanting to distance itself from some of these movements regarding them as 'political' and therefore not only not its direct concern, but with the potential to undermine its status and position in society. It is always a danger for religion to safeguard its right to exist by building alliances with a ruling elite. Hence its tendency too often to want to create a space between its religious activities and those of the state, and when the going gets difficult to be silent, when what it should be doing is to cry out.

Religion may even be inimical or even hostile to some spiritualities out of jealousy, mistakenly seeing them as leeching away its support, becoming critical of insights it cannot fathom, and even openly hostile to what it judges to be a dilution of the treasure to which it thought it had sole rights. Rather it should realise that in these lie the spirituality it needs, and to whose origins every spirituality can be traced if it is to fulfil its role as a vehicle for the worship of God and the service of humankind.

It is not surprising therefore if some have come to regard spirituality as an alternative to religion. Tired of the formulae that no longer seem to connect with their experience, with expressions of belief that seem outmoded and irrelevant, but still reluctant to let go of the meaning that religion at its best had brought to their lives, they have ended up 'believing without belonging'. For others spirituality has become a way of hanging on, of keeping some kind of tenuous connection with the tradition in which they'd been nurtured, while finding their inspiration in parallel practices and complimentary disciplines.

It is sad, because much as spirituality needs religion, religion needs spirituality just as much if it is not to forget that at its core is an encounter with a living God who demands justice not sacrifice. It has been a misreading of spirituality, by those within as well as outside religion, to see it as anti-material and a withdrawal from conflict, to see waiting on God as solely other-worldly and unrealistic. The best of the spiritualities have always made a connection between contemplation of the divine and engagement with the powers on earth, challenging institutional wrongs and organising resistance to forces that threaten to dehumanise the individual and to jeopardise social harmony.

Andrew and Philip, Bartholomew and Matthew, Thomas and James the son of Alphaeus, Thaddaeus and Simon the Zealot, and Judas Iscariot, left at the bottom of the mountain missed out on the drama taking place in the clouds above their heads. Soon they were to find out they'd need Peter, James and John to take them into their secret if they were to carry on.

II

'SHAME ON MY BEARD UNLESS I OPEN THE DOOR TO FIND OUT IF WHAT THEY SAY ABOUT IT IS TRUE'

'ay gwir a dywedir am hynny'

4. Got no Dreaming?:

spirituality as the hope of planet earth

'Ah wretch! Said they, the bird to slay,
That made the breeze to blow!'

To get down to earth, it's odd that first you have to go up. But that's what they did. The four of them. Sometimes together, sometimes alone, sometimes in pairs, climbing up. Hardy types used to the harsh and dusty landscape.

The higher they went the more rugged the terrain. The vegetation more scarce. The rocks brown, and the caves without regular habitation that had once provided shelter for patriots fleeing the massacre of the Seleucid butcher, Antiochus Epiphanes. A hidey-hole for Judas Maccabaeus to rally the resistance. But not enough. Never enough. So the caves became tombs, and memorials of great but futile defiance. Some still harboured wild souls, ostracised or hermit-like, eking out an existence on locusts, wild honey and good will; barefoot in tattered clothing or animal skins. Flesh as rough as leather; scarred, unwashed.

Higher and higher, in the conspiracies of the mountains where secrets are shared and overheard, they pondered and prayed. And at the top, nothing but the panorama of the Davidic kingdom, a holy land. Its distant olive groves and vineyards, its scraggy goats on scraggier pasture, its village communities, its bigger towns. And far away, the sea: that great mystery that provided a living but demanded too many sacrifices; the waves moving, breathing, stretching to infinity, below a sun that was hot and yellow, that ripened and burnt, that came up and as suddenly went down, deserting the earth to cold, starry nights, and a moon that shed a lesser light.

Above them, birds squawked and hunted for signs of life

around the bleak rocks, descending in cruel swoops to squabble over disputed prey. And sometimes rain, but never enough to source the underground cisterns and wet the soil's hard crust. And what there was filtering fitfully down through the fissures in the rock's surface to lose itself eventually in the distant Jordan.

This was their world. In the beginning: God. And Jesus taught them the secret of the earth. That it was good. That they needed to let the soil and the sand run through their souls as it did through their fingers. And he taught them to pray. Thy will be done on earth, because:

'To the Lord belong the earth and everything in it,
the world and all its inhabitants.
For it was he who founded it on the seas
and planted it firm on the waters beneath.'

He taught them that their spirituality was bound up with the ebb and flow of the universe. They shared the same heartbeat. All living things: matter and water, inanimate, animate, it made a whole; a God made whole. All was perfectly balanced.

Not for them to know that humankind would later exploit and abuse, plunder and exhaust what was finite and irreplaceable. That men would fly where only birds flew then, and burrow deep into solid rock, and skim the seas to suck liquid gold from its unfathomable reservoirs, and race across the surface of the earth discharging poison like rampaging skunks.

So the sea levels rise and the coastal populations are now turned from settled communities into migrants roaming across continents to seek alternative livelihoods. Hurricanes come oftener and worse; the dead and the devastation plotting their terrible paths. The flowers and the creatures, little and large, more than a million species by 2050, destined for extinction. The droughts multiplying, with whole tribes immobilised by hunger and disease, and the world's governments unwilling, and the aid agencies unable to cope. The wars worse because the prize is bigger and the weapons more lethal. Wild fires to claim the forests and consume the undergrowth's fleeing life. And it is not good. It is not at all good.

This is of a different order to the fluctuations in cold and heat, that have seen our planet pass through successive climate changes over millions of years. Much of what we are experiencing now is what we ourselves have done. We have created conditions that are not normal and on a scale and at a speed that causes the scientific world to hold its breath. By consuming our inheritance of coal, of oil and gas; by felling the rain forests in our greed for wood to sustain our profligate lifestyle, we twentieth and twenty-first century humans, we late arrivals on planet earth, have upset the balance of Eden.

We have destabilised the eco system, and our planet is now perspiring and slowly suffocating under a duvet of carbon dioxide. Within the last few generations we've indulged in an energy jamboree. First it was the developed countries, and now China and India and the rest of the developing world want their share of this fossil fuel based economy.

Added to unrestrained mining for oil and coal, we've also ripped up the hedgerows to make bigger fields leading to the loss of the wild life that sheltered and nurtured their young in its branches and folds, and we've fished the seas with a thoughtless abandon, endangering not only the shoals that have roamed the deep since the dawn of time, but the birds of the air entangled in the spreading mesh of the fisherman's nets.

We ill-fated inhabitants of these last two centuries have succeeded to the judgement heaped on the head of the unlucky Ancient Mariner in Coleridge's 'Rime', who shot the albatross tracking his boat and brought bad luck on all his crew:

'And I had done an hellish thing,
And it would work 'em woe:

For all averred, I had killed the bird
That made the breeze to blow.'

And now the albatross as a species is bound for extinction and serves as a sign of all the other losses still to come.

'Ah wretch! said they, the bird to slay,
That made the breeze to blow!'

Our children may sing Francis of Assisi's Canticle of the Sun, about 'our sister Mother Earth, who feeds us and rules us, and produces various fruits and flowers and herbs', but they will grow up to rule, not be ruled by, our sister Mother Earth.

This mindless plundering and squandering of earth's resources has largely come about within the last hundred years, which is roughly the same time span, at least among the big spenders, that has seen an increase in humankind's 'spirituality deficit'. As we have lost touch with our spirituality and the spirituality of all created things, we have created and compounded the problem. Humankind stands in the dock not only charged but also found guilty of profligate consumption of the earth's natural but limited resources. Humankind has lost respect for its environment because it has lost sight of the way all living things belong, cohere and hold together.

For the greater part of our time on earth a partnership was possible between humankind and the rest of creation: the land, the sea, the sky the climate. That partnership has broken down within the lifetime of these recent generations, and it has happened at the same time as people have disavowed their essential spirituality. The first crow of the cock to wake us from this dangerous sleep was a United Nations Earth Summit in Rio de Janeiro in 1992 which urged its member states 'to search for a sustainable future'. But not many were roused. More turned over to sleep on.

We have lost that sense of the earth and all it represents as a sacred trust, to be enjoyed certainly, and to be harvested, but not to be used thoughtlessly, selfishly as if we could discard it when we've finished with it because we think there must be a replacement somewhere in the universe as there is for everything else we make and throw away when it's empty or broke. Only this time there is no replacement. This is it, and when we've used it up, it's gone!

One of the few places now left on earth where there is still an innate sense of the sacredness of the land and the obligation of its human tenants is among the aborigines of Australia. It may be a Stone Age culture, but its tribes have retrained a memory that we would do well to recover.

As they gather around the huge rock of Mount Uluru in the mulga strewn wilderness at the world's red centre, they see holy ground not the geological freak the incomers renamed Ayer's Rock. As the sun's 'dreaming' from east to west plays on its sandstone flanks, staining it from reddish brown to brilliant red, from cobalt blue to crimson purple, it comes alive for them with the life of all that is, and is forever something to be respected and venerated, not to be climbed and conquered.

For these people land is not something to be owned and possessed, to be staked out and claimed with boundaries and fences, dividing neighbours and nations. Rather it is to be respected and revered, and our life journeys as tribes or alone, the 'Dreaming', the 'Songlines' of our existence, should be seen as constantly crossing and criss-crossing, but never enclosing.

'White man got no Dreaming
Him go 'nother way.'

was the stark conclusion of the tribal leader, Muta a Murinbata, as he watched the settlers from across the sea establish their communities, imposing their laws,

'White man him go different
Him go road belong himself.'

The moral dilemma now facing us is further refined by the realisation that human exploitation of the earth is not only extensive but very one sided with far reaching consequences as far as the poor, under developed world is concerned. The cock had crowed at least once before that significant Earth Summit when a former prime minister of Norway, Gro Harlem Brundtland, had warned that desperately poor people do desperate things to their immediate environment. Global poverty thus becomes both the cause and the victim of its destiny.

Twenty years later the cock crowed a third time, when another United Nations survey concluded that the situation had got worse and that the gap between the well off and the poor had never been wider. Not only had personal wealth in the richest countries grown by a third over those last two decades but the natural capital on which so much human well-being and economic activity depends: water, land, the air and the atmosphere, biodiversity and marine resources, had also declined.

'Ah wretch! said they, the bird to slay,
That made the breeze to blow!'

Global warming as an explanation for climatic changes may continue to divide the scientific community, but for those like this author, who are persuaded, warnings such as that issued by the Parliament of the World's Religions, meeting in Chicago in 1993, cannot be lightly set aside. According to the Parliament's communiqué, there can be 'no global order without a new global ethic' which, in turn, 'involves promoting sustainable value systems'. Al Gore, Nobel peace laureate and former vice-president of the United States made the same point in his 2006 documentary feature film, 'An Inconvenient Truth'. 'We can no longer afford to view global warming as a political issue,' Gore warned, 'rather it is the biggest moral challenge facing our global civilization.'

Moral dilemmas, however, are the stuff of which religion is made. And if religion cannot rise to the biggest challenge of our time, of what use is it? Religion's contribution to date, however, has been somewhat of a mixed bag. On the positive side is the place given to respecting natural resources in all the sacred writings. The world's faiths all teach that the planet and its myriad life forms, plant and animal, in the ocean depth, on the surface of the earth, in the air above, from the most rudimentary molecular structure to the highest form of intelligent life, are inter-dependent. That the powerful of creation are to be its servants, surveyors of its stock and its stewards, even to the infinity of space.

The teaching of the Buddha affirms that all life is interrelated, that nothing exists in isolation, independent of all other life; that every being and phenomenon exists or occurs only because of its relationship with other beings or phenomena, even if a less spiritually enlightened generation only pays it lip service. The Torah promises that 'While the earth lasts seedtime and harvest, cold and heat, summer and winter, day and night shall never cease,' but its Jewish and Christian readers have conveniently forgotten that it was a promise based on humankind also keeping its side of the bargain to respect the creation. And those who spun the ancient tales of Brân and of Branwen, of myth and magic, of entrancements and spells, were those who knew that earth and the elements were subject to ultimate values, and that to cross them incurred calamity and loss.

On the mountainside in the Syrian uplands, when the four friends stopped to pray it would be with psalms of praise to the author and sustainer of this creation, and not in general but in specific terms:

'Praise the Lord from the earth,
you sea monsters and ocean depths.'

Theirs was a faith that marvelled at the detail and how God had fashioned human kind out of the primordial mud.

'What is a frail mortal, that you should be mindful of him
a human being, that you should take notice of him?
Yet you have made him little less than a god.'

Theirs was a belief that the wild flowers were 'better dressed than Solomon with all his beads and bangles!'

'You crown the year with your good gifts;
places where you have passed drip with plenty.'

Theirs was a creed that saw the destiny of creation bound up with the destiny of humankind; that creation needed a human response if it was to be the beautiful spinning planet intended at the command 'let there be light' at the dawn of time:

'If I lift up my eyes to the hills,
where shall I find help?
My help comes only from the Lord,
maker of heaven and earth.'

After they'd prayed they would talk and revisit the history of their people with Jesus telling them not to sneer at the tale of the Syrian who'd once crossed the mountains of Lebanon to take back with him to Damascus soil from their homeland so he could be nearer to their God. Naaman: a grand courtier blighted by disease and made well in their Jordan River. His may have been a primitive faith which belonged to a time when every country had its god, or so it seemed, but it treasured a truth that did not date; that to reach God you had to feel for God through solid earth. As the memory of God has receded further, so has our respect for the earth and the waters that cover the earth that were once regarded as the gateway to heaven, with God as their protector.

In their writings and their teachings the great religions have all affirmed the unique place of the environment in the progress and wellbeing of humankind. At the same time religion, of itself, cannot disclaim responsibility for the part it has also played in contributing to the problem. Christianity more than any other faith has to accept a larger share of blame in this respect, since it is the faith that has predominated in the developed world and fuelled its unrestrained entrepreneurship. Some go further, arguing that Protestant Christianity stands particularly condemned because of its insistence on human helplessness in the face of Divine generosity, thus leaving it with no theology of nature to temper the injunction in Genesis for humankind to rule and exercise dominion over creation.

Like the Ancient Mariner's shipmates we have conveniently forgotten the lessons of adversity when the warnings have seemed premature, exaggerated or mistaken:

'Twas right, said they, such birds to slay
That bring the fog and mist.'

Those religions with a linear sense of history, of the time span of creation having a definite beginning and end, have also been particularly prone to accepting a doomsday scenario. Some have argued that no change of course is necessary, because it's all predestined. Others have argued that far from any change being necessary we must take positive action to hasten the end, thereby ushering in the grand climax in which the good will be rewarded and the evil consigned to hell.

For some people, films like the cult movie, 'The Day after Tomorrow' are not just science-fiction but manna from heaven, and the words of historians like Eric Hosbawm that, 'We have reached a point of historic crisis,' proof positive that we have come to the end of the road, since 'the forces generated by the techno-scientific economy are now great enough to destroy the environment, i.e. the natural foundations of human life.'

Sometimes the human species needs to be frightened into taking action, but the danger is that it can result in a kind of paralysis where nobody even tries to do anything to avert the disaster. It can also fuel the distorted logic of extremist fundamentalist believers who take these predictions as their cue to precipitate the very end the scientists believe we can still avert.

Even the more moderate voices within the churches have found themselves drawn into the slough of despair, warning that, 'The earth is in peril. Our only home is in plain jeopardy. We are at the precipice of self destruction,' with three of the Apocalypse's four horsemen already on the horizon: harbingers of war, famine and destruction.

The most dire scientific diagnosis of the environment's condition, however, has always added the caveat that all is not lost, that we can still reverse the worst effects of pollution, that something can be done to get the planet back on course, with one expert even holding out the prospect of world peace if humankind would only act 'as a species' for the first time for its own good 'as a species'.

Where religion as a formal discipline has thus often failed humanity in its engagement with its environment, spirituality has a much better record, because it has been free to tap into concepts and values that resonate with the human spirit. It prevents the material and the spiritual being pitted against each other like combatants in which one must win at the expense of the other, holding instead to the fundamental unity of both.

While therefore religion has had an uneven record in addressing the issue that is now probably one of the biggest facing humankind, it will be the restoration of spirituality that will contribute to the planet's healing. According to a remarkable but unknown mediaeval monk, spirituality of this kind is so down to earth that it can imagine God saying:

'I am the wind that breathes upon the sea,
I am the wave on the ocean,
I am the murmur of leaves rustling,
I am the rays of the sun,'

Seven hundred year later another monk, the mystic Thomas Merton, could write in similar vein that, 'Creation had been given to men as a clear window through which the light of God would shine into men's souls.'

'I am the beam of the moon and stars,
I am the power of trees growing,
I am the bud breaking into blossom,
I am the movement of the salmon swimming',

- says God; and the mystic replies: 'Sun and moon, night and day, rain and sun, the cross, the flowering tree, all these things were transparent. They spoke to man not of themselves, but of him who made them.'

'I am the courage of the wild boar fighting,
I am the speed of the stag running,
I am the strength of the ox pulling the plough,
I am the size of the mighty oak tree,'

When Llywellyn was Prince in Gwynedd, the unknown monk wrote with a large hand, in what has become the oldest manuscript in the Welsh tongue, the Black Book of Carmarthen, that God said:

'I am the thoughts of all people
Who praise my beauty and grace.'

It is this transparency that we will need to reclaim if we are to
correct the spirituality deficit that has contributed to so much
environmental damage in the first place. A transparency which is
not pantheism which confuses the creation with the creator, but
pan-en-theism, seeing God in all things and seeing all things in
God. Theirs was an earthy faith; a spirituality that was serious
about land. 'You are our breath,' wrote the twentieth century
Quaker poet, Waldo:

'You are the flight
Of our longing to the depths of heaven...
You are the moment of light,
Whose aura embraces our life'

Unless we can recover the same earthiness, however high or
remote the mountains we climb, we will go on being disap-
pointed, and the planet will remain in its pain.

Reverence for Life was Albert Schweitzer's name for it.
Schweitzer, who held doctorates in medicine, music and theology,
with his colonial hat and drooping moustache, bent double over a
hole in the ground in a clearing at the heart of Africa, reaching
down to rescue any little creature that might be trapped there
before giving permission for the heavy posts to be lowered that
would form the foundation of his hospital in Lambarene.
Schweitzer, the Franco-German missionary who could make the
organ of St. Sulpice in Paris throb and tingle to Bach's Toccata and
Fugue in D minor, showing that respect for life, for all that
breathes, was no idle philosophy but a total way of life.

More recently, the scientists James Lovelock and Lynn
Margulis came up with their own version of what is essentially
another spiritual response to the environment. What they say

about the planet's surface conditions always being conducive to the life forms that inhabit it, led to the novelist, William Golding, persuading Lovelock to call their interpretation 'Gaia', after the Greek goddess who brought life form out chaos. Gaia comes very close to integrating not only the different earth sciences, but sets them in a perspective that is spiritual. It's a theory that sits comfortably with the spirituality of that other mediaeval mystic, the abbess Hildergard of Bingen, for whom, as in the Celtic tradition, nature was the visible face of God:

'I am the breeze that nurtures all things green ...
I am the rain coming from the dew that causes the grasses to laugh
with the joy of life.'

Those who challenge us to act now to save the planet are, however, sufficiently realistic to recognise that there will be no easy solutions, even for those who accept that the issue is as much spiritual as it is moral. It's a dilemma that was played out unexpectedly on a macro scale in 2007 when a Hindu community in West Wales clashed with local farmers over what to do about a sick cow. In her sympathetic 'Elegy for Shambo', Gwyneth Lewis wrote:

'Every good farmer knows that his herd
Is holy. He will protect it, his mother.
If one bull's sacred, then so are all others.'

It became international news overnight. Government agencies invoked court orders, the police were enlisted and monks and nuns of the Many Names of God commune in the Skanda Vale prayed while the television crews beamed the story round the world. Shambo, a Friesian bull, garlanded and guarded had become an unlikely cause celebre in an environmental dispute involving religion.

Farmers, reeling from an earlier Foot and Mouth epidemic feared for their remaining stocks if Shambo had contracted tuberculosis and wanted him culled. The Hindus in obedience to Krishna's teaching in the Bhagavad-Gita of service to life and devotion to God believed that he could be treated and saved:

'If one bull's sacred, then so are all others.'

In the end, Shambo had to go. But there were no winners. The action taken followed the accepted Western practice in dealing with infectious diseases in animals. It was the best that could be done under the circumstances. And it will be no different as we tackle the greater environmental threat of global warming. We won't always get it right. But unless we reclaim the spiritual aspect of the issue, we may never have the chance.

What matters are not the flaws, natural or of human origin, that beset the planet, but earth's potential to recover its destiny through human inter-action. It has been, and still is, a victim of the breakdown between matter and spirit. And we, insignificant creatures in one sense, but with such magnificent potential in another, can, by taking responsibility for our own carbon footprints, begin to right the scales. At the end of his narrative, the Ancient Mariner's advice, born of painful, personal experience is that:

'He prayeth well, who loveth well
Both man and bird and beast.'

As Peter, James and John made their way down from the mountain, Jesus taught them to pray, Thy will be done on earth. And it crossed their minds as they clambered over the rocks towards the softer, flatter plain, that they might just have seen the fourth horseman, but not yet with a crown.

5. An unacknowledged barrier:
the helplessness of religion in the face
of systemic evil

'the tree of knowledge is the genius of our blind science.'

On their free evenings the staff cars would drive them the eight kilometre journey down into the city. With their distinctive uniforms they would expect the most prominent, or the most discreet, tables at favoured restaurants, and the best seats in the house to watch plays by the national theatre company, or enjoy concerts from the School of Music. In the art galleries and museums they could admire some of the best collections in Europe. And in the bars, the beer gardens, and the brothels, to dispense with rank.

For the aesthetes and those who aspired to join their number, Buchenwald was a good posting because of its proximity to so much culture and history. Goethe and Schiller, prophets of the enlightenment, had shared artistic insights with each other as they strolled up the Ettersberg. Over cake and coffee in the city's numerous cafes they held their followers spellbound with heated talk on the finer points of humanism and theology, science and painting.

Bach had brought the city's honest, and not so honest, worshippers to the very gates of heaven with his fugues and cantatas, and Liszt had made music in the concert halls of the Duchy's capital. It was here at the end of the First World War, because Berlin was in turmoil, that a defeated nation had signed the constitution that would give them the Weimar Republic. A republic that saw the flowering of a German culture to enrich the world with the philosophy of Martin Heidegger, the novels of Thomas Mann and the plays of Bertolt Brecht.

From time to time, of course, there would be veiled talk about what exactly went on in the barbed wire settlement perched on the hillside overlooking the city, because there were provisions to be delivered to the camp and the traders would notice things and hear things. But this was a time of war. And in war even the most civilized nation could not afford to be lenient with enemies of the state. 'Jedem das Seine' was written in iron letters on its gates: 'To each his due'. They wouldn't be there if they hadn't done something wrong.

Later the good citizens of Weimar, and of the World, would learn that a quarter of a million prisoners had passed through those gates: Russians, Poles and Czechs; French, Belgian and Dutch; Spaniards and Italians, Danes and Norwegians, as well as Germans. Men, women and children, their identities emasculated to no more than a number on a metal tag dangling from their necks. Fifty-six thousand of them had died from beatings, starvations, executions and 'experiments': communists and Jews, gays and gypsies, believers and sceptics. Among them was the Austrian Catholic priest Otto Neururer, beatified by Pope John Paul II. Arrested for refusing to sanction the marriage of a Nazi divorcee, Fr Otto was hanged for baptising a fellow prisoner. Forty years later I saw that someone had left a bunch of fresh chrysanthemums on his cell door.

Over schnapps in the city's hostelries late into the night SS officers would outdo each other with callous boasts, while some with troubled consciences would seek out confessors they hoped they could trust.

There were many good people in Weimar, as there were in the rest of Germany, often with a highly developed spirituality. Many of these were becoming increasingly troubled by the stories of what went on in the camp outside the city's walls. A few spoke out and disappeared. Some were frightened into perpetual silence. It would take Ionescu's theatre of the absurd to help them later to hear the question, if not to know how to give the answer: Why had we allowed it to happen? Since then the world has had to face the same eerie question over Bosnia, Rwanda, Darfur, and too many more, and been equally baffled by its failure to give an answer.

What is this dark cloud that descends on a whole people to render them incapable of accessing their decent feelings? That makes them mute when their consciences cry out for them to shout that this shall not be? What strange enchantment paralyses the memory to suppress the human spirit's inherent goodness? What, asks the poet and critic Alan Llwyd, turns good people for the most part, into:

' ... *mad worshippers before the altars of the Fuhrer's mass performing the devil's rite, exalting the beast and the boar's progeny'?*

Can there be some concentrations of evil, so repetitive and inter-connected, so intense and depraved, that they form an unacknowledged barrier that few can ever progress beyond them? Evils that have been refined by human inventiveness to become more terrible, because:

*'In the Eden of modern technology scientific experiments are the apple,
and the tree of knowledge is the genius of our blind science.'*

When the friends came down from the mountain, they were heady with what they'd experienced. Each was deep in his own thoughts, Peter turning over the moment, James trying to make sense of the experience, John knowing that because of it they'd never be the same again, and Jesus surer, clearer, more aware of his destiny. Peter was wanting to tell the others, and also not wanting, because he wouldn't be able to explain it. He knew it wouldn't make sense to those who hadn't been there, seen, heard or engaged with it. Coming out of a very private, intense experience of pure spirituality, they discovered the world as messy as they'd left it all those days - those aeons - ago, and their companions unchanged, if a bit distant because they'd been left behind to deal with the man who'd brought his epileptic child for Jesus to heal, except that Jesus wasn't there. He'd gone away to pray and they didn't know when he'd be back. He'd been known to go off for six weeks at a stretch sometimes!

The boy's father had been loath to give up and return home empty handed having come so far. The consultant may be away, but at least most of his team were still around. Why not get them to put their training to good use to make the lad better. That's what was expected of disciples. They learnt from watching their tutor. He shared with them the mysteries of his secret arts so they could become experts in their own right.

They'd done their best. But it hadn't been good enough. Philip and Thomas were less surprised. There were things Jesus could do they didn't understand, but they accepted the evidence of their eyes. They weren't so sure though that these powers were that transferrable. When Jesus talked about God, for instance, God came across as very real, even personal. But who'd ever seen God? He, Philip, definitely hadn't! Jesus was certainly everything they'd been led to expect in the Mosaic tradition and by the prophets, and more. But he'd have liked it if Jesus could make God as real for them, as he was for him.

Philip's mate, Nathaniel, had taken a bit of convincing at first that a messianic figure could ever emerge from a dump like Nazareth, until that is he'd met Jesus. Then Nathaniel had become as devoted a follower as any of them. And, just then, was trying his level best to help with the boy's healing.

The boy was sick and his father desperate. This had been his last hope, but he couldn't hang around for days, perhaps weeks, waiting. He'd the rest of the family to think about. He'd a job to be getting on with. Jesus had a reputation. That's why he'd come.

Thomas was watching all their efforts with a detachment that

Nathaniel found exasperating. Thomas had the kind of temperament that needed to know the end plan if he was to give his best day to day. He could see the significance of Jesus' healing ministry in re-enforcing his mission, but the goal was less distinct. There were hints in some of the things Jesus had been saying lately that troubled him too. Ruth, Thomas's twin, seemed more ready to live a day at a time, though her sharp mind had picked out things in Jesus's interpretation of their scriptures that Thomas seemed to have missed; things that made her more prepared to think the unthinkable, that he'd be cruelly treated, that the leaders of all the religious groups would turn against him, even that he'd be killed. Thomas perhaps hadn't wanted to hear.

And then when all was confusion, incrimination and impotence, the man angry and frustrated, Jesus turned up. He was there as large as life, and in total command. Why the commotion? he asked in assumed innocence. 'He's my only child,' the father chipped in, 'and he's plagued by convulsions. I asked your assistants to help him but they didn't know what to do.' And where the assistants had failed, Jesus succeeded. Embarrassment for the assistants. Gratitude from the father. Surprise from the boy. And applause from the crowd.

When everything had died down and the last of the onlookers had left, it was Philip who asked the crucial question. Why couldn't we do it? We prayed, we believed. Didn't we pray hard enough? Didn't we have enough faith? And Jesus' answer was not what Philip or any of them had expected. Instead of blaming them, he denounced the times in which they lived: 'What an unbelieving and perverse generation'. Not what unbelieving companions I have, but what a perverse generation. The unacknowledged barrier was not *in* them, but *around* them, and it was strong enough, dense enough to block off their capacity to respond to human need with the compassion of which they were capable.

For Jesus faith had never been an issue of consent to certain indisputable propositions about the inalienable nature of God. That was what religion required. To cross the 't's and dot the 'i's. To know who could be included. Who could be eligible for the benefits. That might make sense to the Pharisees and Sadducees, but it left him cold. It was far too mechanistic, too unspiritual. For him, faith was a relationship of hope and trust in the Other, not a belief *that*, but a belief *in*. It was because hope and trust in that sense was no longer current in their culture or their times, that the nine had been handicapped in their efforts to help the boy. It was a lesson they needed to learn because theirs was to be a battle with principalities and powers, which might take temporal form but belonged to that larger struggle between good and evil.

When we look at a Buchenwald or a Belsen, a Rwanda or a Darfur, and ask ourselves: How can such things happen? Why don't good people prevent them? Why doesn't God intervene? It is because we have not recognised the force of that analysis, that the faithlessness of a generation can have an insidious effect on even the best of that generation. The role and effect of the culture on our capacity to do good, and the power of evil to stifle the genuine spirituality that courses through most people's veins, can never be underestimated.

For the seven legendary figures in the old Celtic tale it had led to a collective loss of memory, only the remembrance wasn't completely obliterated. 'All the sorrow they had themselves seen and suffered, they remembered none of it, nor any of the grief in the world.' Nevertheless something still lingered under the surface to recur in nightmares that could not be recalled when dawn, or the face of their dead Queen's half-brother, Efnysien, startled them from sleep. Sometimes there were horses that rode across their slumbers. The grooms mopping up the blood. Fine Irish stallions, the perspiration gleaming on their steaming flanks, nostrils flared as they galloped with the speed of the wind. Of doors opening and closing; only the third was never unlocked.

Then one of the seven breaks the eighty year spell. 'Shame on my beard,' he swears, 'unless I open the door to find out if what they say about it is true.' 'And when he looked, every loss they had ever suffered, and every kinsman and companion they had lost, and every ill that had befallen them was as clear as if they had encountered it in that very place.'

The tale taps into the very earliest awareness of human kind that knowledge carries with it responsibility. It's the Garden of Eden, it's Pandora's Box, it's the clash of selective ignorance versus painful but inescapable reality, it's:

> ' ... *the hole*
> *in God's side that is the wound*
> *of knowledge'*

in R S Thomas's poem about the thirteenth century Fransiscan, Roger Bacon. Germany's confessing church theologian, Dietrich Bonhoeffer, held in Buchenwald and hanged in Flossenburg, called it our 'coming of age'. It is that moment of enlightenment when we have to let go of a childish concept of God, of a divine superman who swoops in and out of our lives selectively to save some (usually us) from the worst excesses of human folly and wickedness. We have to face the truth, and confront it.

This tension between wanting and not wanting to know, was also part of the scenario played out on the mountainside above Caesarea Philippi. Transported by their vision of Jesus in relation to Moses and Elijah, the two archetypal figures of their people, Peter, James and John wanted to seal the moment in aspic, to capture the present so that it became eternal, to sustain forever the exquisite sensation of heaven on earth, because what else does Peter's proposal to put up dwellings for them all mean?

They had families they loved, friends they cared about and livelihoods that others depended on. In that moment, though, when time collapsed and sights, sounds, smells, feelings where heightened, nothing else mattered. This was the most superb spirituality. This was the most complete harmony between earth and heaven. This was the weightlessness of souls in free fall.

When the story got out, some said Peter had spoken thoughtlessly. That in the aftermath of a theophany he'd blurted out the first thing that came into his head. But that is to miss the point. Peter knew exactly what he was saying, because he knew what he was feeling. He also knew, no sooner had the words passed his lips, not only that it could not be, but that because it had happened, from then on, for him, for James and John, for the nine waiting their return, everything would be different, everything had to be different.

They had touched the heights and it had given a depth to their understanding of what needed to be accomplished and at what cost if the world too was to be transfigured. It had opened a door for them, 'and every loss they had ever suffered, and every kinsman and companion they had lost, and every ill that had befallen them was as clear as if they had encountered it in that place'. And their recollection afterwards, when they told of their time on the mountain to their nine companions, was that Moses and Elijah had spoken of Jesus's departure and his destiny, and that their departure and destiny was bound up with his.

> 'Share your secret, Peter, how
> The Holy Spirit came to disturb the house...
> The bolt of the door facing the street was opened
> And God's message was hurled through a crooked world.'

Spirituality is often thought of and defined as affecting the human spirit as opposed to material or physical things. But it is not 'as opposed to'. Rather it is 'in the interests of' material and physical things. This notion of a dichotomy between the flesh and the spirit is false. We are not either physical or spiritual beings, we are both. It is our spirituality that refines and perfects our physical and material being and demands that we take the real and often pained physical world seriously.

Bernini's sculpture, The Ecstasy of St Theresa, imprisoned behind a phalanx of intrusive candlesticks in its niche in the Cornaro Chapel of the church of Santa Maria della Vittoria in Rome, was and remains both scandalous and fascinating because it blurs the edges between the physical and the spiritual. Theresa is captured in the sleep of God, the transfiguring coma in which the mystics glimpsed the eternal glory, but Bernini has given her an orgasmic expression and the figure at her side, spear erect, more lover than angel. Its spirituality engages because it is so real, because it says flesh and blood can also know what it is to be divine. It depicts the intensive edge between something that is both exquisite and agony.

The spirituality in every world religion that speaks most loudly to the human condition is the one that doesn't divorce the pain from the joy; that recognises the imperfections, the flaws and the wounds inherent in life, and engages with it realistically and redemptively. It resists the temptation to withdraw, or to wash one's hands of the blood, and still seeks to find a way or ways of reviving hope. It redeems without rejecting.

Jesus had taught his followers neither to reject their culture, nor to accept it as it was. It may be, it was, imperfect, but it could be transformed, it should be redeemed. He'd reminded them of the time Elijah's successor, Elisha, was travelling through the Jordan valley with his coterie of disciples and had stopped to eat. But the land was in the grip of a drought. Hungry and weary Elisha's little band of prophets had scrabbled and scoured the arid landscape for anything they could pick or pull up to make into a broth. One by one they had returned with their meagre pickings: a few surviving tendrils here, some scrawny roots there, and little more. But it made a meal and would assuage, if not satisfy their empty bellies.

Then the cry had gone up from one and all as they gulped

their first mouthfuls: 'Man of God, there is death in the pot.' It was not only inedible, it was poisonous. Elisha thought he detected the flavour of the wild pumpkin that was ideal in small quantities for medicine, but toxic in excess. They were all for pouring the broth away. Better to sleep hungry than be ill. But the prophet remembered an antidote from his childhood. He added a little flour, and he stirred it in, and by and by the toxicity was neutralised and they were able to eat and be satisfied.

And that's how it must be with you, Jesus had explained. Identify the ills of society, but do not reject it. Do not turn your back on it to pursue some personal salvation in isolation from those around you. You won't find it. Rather, see what you can add to the cultural brew that will make it palatable again. But he warned them it would be costly, because to face the reality of what was wrong, to open the third door of the Celtic folk tale, would mean confronting 'every loss they had ever suffered, and every kinsman and companion they had lost, and every ill that had befallen them.'

For the seven survivors in their island limbo it meant confronting Efnysien, or rather the memory of what he'd done. Efnysien: Branwen's strange half brother who idolised her, and was in love with her, disputed Brân's right to marry her off to the Irish king. 'Is that what they have done with such a fine maiden,' was his startled reaction on finding out Branwen was already wed, 'and my sister at that, given her away without my permission?' And he'd taken his terrible revenge. He'd gone for the Irish king's horses, 'and cut their lips to the teeth, and their ears down to their heads, and their tails to their backs; and where he could not get a grip on the eyelids, he cut them to the bone. In that way,' the ancient story teller concluded, 'he maimed the horses, so they were no good for anything.' And in Buchenwald and all the other dark places where folk hide from the light, they would do the same and worse, only not to horses but people.

Into this maelstrom of apparently unending and unmentionable acts, Jesus offers something unique. He offers forgiveness. The forgiveness that confronts and exposes, that requires punishment, but that offers redemption; that breaks through the unacknowledged barrier that provides a cloak of respectability to what lies hidden, and which religion then and now has too often failed to offer because it has thought its best interests lay with, rather than against, Caesar.

So when he healed, Jesus would pronounce forgiveness. Forgiveness because the times were sick, not forgiveness for the victim alone, but for the condition, the circumstances that had produced and created it. The culture may be faithless, it may disempower many who might otherwise be able to resist and overcome its negative influences, but it is not beyond hope, because God cares. In Bonhoeffer's beautiful verse prayed in a Buchenwald cell:

'God goeth to every man when sore bestead,
Feedeth body and spirit with his bread,
For Christians, heathen alike he hangeth dead:
And both alike forgiving.'

Forgiveness may be the defining description of Christian spirituality, but it would be foolish to deny its presence and its influence in other world faiths too. Islam teaches the importance of basing human relations on forgiveness because, 'We cannot expect Allah's forgiveness unless we also forgive those who do wrong to us.' Rosh Hashanah, in the Jewish faith, not only marks the New Year, but also God's forgiveness of Adam and Eve for their disobedience in eating the forbidden fruit. And the Buddhist Lama, Surya Das, often counsels his students 'not to forgive and forget, but to forgive and remember.'

Sometimes it even makes an appearance in the most unlikely of places. In an episode of the television series 'Dr Who', where the two time lords who represent good and evil confront each other in a cosmic fight to the finish, the good Doctor tells his defeated foe: 'I forgive you'! It is all the more startling because of the context; it emerges in a piece of popular everyday culture. It slips into the public consciousness, buffeted and blunted by news of great evils, with a message that redemption is still possible, and that the unlikely key is forgiveness. Though religion's responses may be muted, spirituality keeps the door open to the power of forgiveness to confront and to heal. The message of the Sunday Schools, Dr Who script writer Russell T Davies had spent his childhood avoiding, had nevertheless taken root in his restless mind.

Forgiveness is the spiritual ingredient that draws the sting of evil. To forgive is never to forget Buchenwald and Auschwitz, Hiroshima and Nagasaki, Rwanda and Darfur, and all the other dark places of the earth. Rather it is to remember them with such intensity that we act to change those aspects of our culture that can give rise to further suffering. That we acknowledge what has been unacknowledged, and, by acknowledging, deprive it of its ability to disempower.

In her spiritual autobiography, Sheila Cassidy, the young medical doctor arrested and tortured by the military Junta in Chile following the assassination of President Salvador Allende, depicts this act of acknowledgement as an exercise in stillness. For her, as for the Elijah who appeared at Jesus's side, spirituality's power lies not in gales, earthquakes or peals of thunder, but in still small voices. 'When people ask me what I pray for,' Cassidy explained, 'I say I don't pray for anything; I pray because God is. I sit before him open like an empty bowl, like a flower, like a wound. I give him my joy, my confusion, my boredom, my pain, just lay it there on the floor for him to process as he wishes and when he is ready ...'

'Jedem das Seine' it said in iron letters on the gate above the camp outside Weimar. 'To each his due'. And it was true. But not in the way they meant.

6. Awareness to awareness: spirituality as the antidote to racism

'the flame
of a force which only the black man knows.'

'Eleven o'clock on a Sunday morning is the most segregated hour in America,' Dr Charles W Ward, minister of First Baptist, patiently explained, as I tried to make sense of the existence of two First Baptist churches, both with prominent steeples, within a stone's throw of each other in North Carolina's state capital, Raleigh. That was then, and now is now. But it does not seem to have changed much.

Dr Ward's red brick sanctuary was on South Wilmington Street. The other, a white stone edifice on North Salisbury Street, had North Carolina's minister of Agriculture on its board, and a judge or two in its pews. One was clearly more first than the other!

Charles Ward, ordained by the father of the great civil rights leader Martin Luther King, was far from hopeful about the racial situation in his country. Luther King Jr may have mesmerised a nation and inspired his own people with a dream that has echoed down the years, that his 'four little children will one day live in a nation where they will not be judged by the colour of their skin but by the content of their character', but it didn't feel like it in the southern states. In nearby Greensborough a recent trial of Klu Klux Klan members for the murder of four black Americans had resulted in acquittal, and the state had been reluctant to follow President Carter's lead to appoint blacks to the federal bench.

Twenty years later when tropical storm Alberto hit Florida's prosperous west coast the response was significantly different to the one received months earlier by the black survivors of hurricane Katrina in New Orleans.

Reaching deep into the well of the spirituality that sustained Pastor Ward in those uncertain times, this gracious, thoughtful man added quietly, 'I find the great thing in this world is not so much where we stand as in what direction we are moving.' At the time I wanted to disagree, arguing that it's precisely where we stand, and not the direction in which we're moving, that is all important. I'm not so certain now.

Claiming their new found freedom after the civil war, some black members at North Salisbury Street had gone off to form their own congregation. Others had stayed on, black and white together, but now more white than black. Nevertheless I found the existence of those two communities within a few blocks of each other profoundly sad.

Sad, not because there was an enmity between them; clearly there wasn't, and as far as I could make out they were on the best of terms and respected each other. What was sad was that it institutionalised the concept of separate development based on race.

This is not the same as that freedom of expression that is basic to human communities where in worship some will be looking for inspiration through the beauty of a familiar liturgy and others the spontaneity of song and dance; where some will want a homily that's short and to the point, while others will be expecting nothing less than a long expository sermon; or where the cohesive element is language in a different linguistic majority. Variations of that kind are legitimate and essential.

On the other hand, the variety that is worrying and potentially dangerous is that which is based on race, which typecasts individuals regardless of their aptitudes or gifts, their interests or experiences, making race alone the absolute and deciding factor. The North Salisbury-South Wilmington situation was sad too because it complied with, rather than challenged, the racial divide that is still a factor of life in a nation with such otherwise high ideals. The huddled masses yearning to be free may no longer be slaves, but were still underdogs, and the appeal of the American politician Barack Obama, the product of a Kenyan father and a white mother from Kansas, was that he represented a way in which that racial divide, running like a fault line through American society, might finally be put to rest. In a memorable speech delivered in Philadelphia, Pennsylvania in 2007, Obama reminded his audience 'that we may have different stories, but we hold common hopes; we may not look the same and may not have come from the same place, but we all want to move in the same direction – towards a better future for our children and grandchildren.'

And it was sad because it was institutionalised in religion. Religious communities, based as they are on the oneness of the human family should be the last places to tolerate separate development. That they often do is an indication of religion's failure in this most fundamental area of human rights. The heart of religion may speak and preach equality, but its institutions have become too entwined with a different cultural dynamic, their voice muted and ineffectual.

Visitors to the States are often shocked to find racism still endemic because it is not what they expect. After the civil war, after the Rosa Parks protest, after the laws to desegregate the country, they had thought the matter resolved. But it's still there, contributing to civil unrest as well as an abiding indictment of the inadequacy of religion.

The black African poet, Dombara, captured the latent outrage of his black brother, beaten and kicked by the white man, in these searing lines:

'In his steady eyes there kindled the flame
of a force which only the black man knows.'

It is institutional religion's failure to sell equality to nation states that is the abiding tragedy, especially as religion, in theory at least, has the ideology and the networking to influence and to bring about change. Instead, it too often becomes compromised by the weakness of its own convictions.

Britain's racist inheritance required that it came to terms with its involvement in the slave trade; one of the most disgraceful factors in its history from the sixteenth to the nineteenth centuries. That other European states were also involved doesn't lessen the guilt, nor that there were tribal chiefs on Africa's eastern seaboard willing to barter some of their own kind for the white man's worthless trinkets. Britain was in the forefront of capturing native Africans and transporting them in appalling conditions across a cruel sea to work the empire's sugar plantations on its West Indian colonies where they were treated with wicked inhumanity.

Nor can it be argued any longer that this was a trade that was isolated around the main ports of Bristol and Liverpool. The whole country was involved, from making the chains and the fetters, to enjoying the economic benefits of those little granules of brown and white sugar: a trade sustained and supported for too long by institutional religion. The evangelical poet, William Cowper, exposed the hypocrisy when he wrote of the slaves:

'I pity them greatly, but I must be mum,
For how could we do without sugar and rum?
Especially sugar, so needful we see,
What? give up our desserts, our coffee and tea!'

Even after the abolition of the slave trade by the country's parliament, and generations of immigrants from an empire that had evolved into a commonwealth had been welcomed to its shores to sustain its infrastructure, especially in transport and health, racism still persists as a fact of life in Britain. The 2007 bicentennial celebrations to mark the end of slavery were marred by a spate of fatal stabbings of black youths and racial unrest in some of the country's big cities from Swansea to Glasgow, from

Bristol to Bradford, from London to Leicester. 'How long, O Lord, how long?'

Nor is it something peculiar to Northern Europe and North America, or to countries with a Christian heritage. It's a world-wide phenomenon. Too often racism has ensnared the prevailing religion in support of its ethnic conflicts. Israeli and Palestinian, Turk and Armenian, Russian and Chechen, Hutu and Tutsi, Sunni and Shia, Indian and Pakistani, Orthodox and Muslim, Catholic and Protestant; the list of ethnic conflict is endless; white on white, black on black, white on black, black on white.

Our world is damaged and scarred, wounded and destabilised by racism, and institutional religion has proved virtually helpless to tame this instinct to brand a fellow human being as inferior and to systematise it in terms of colour or caste.

Religion's compliance in racial segregation reached its deplorable apogee in South Africa's twentieth century apartheid regime. There, despite the genetic biologists warning that 'there is no basis in the human genetic code for the notion that skin colour will be predictive of intelligence', and that 'skin colour as a surrogate for race is a social and not a scientific concept', a system of separate development was not only national policy, but reinforced by the Dutch Reformed Church.

With this kind of record it's a matter of some amazement that so many of the voices raised against racism, in all its forms and in all societies, have been the religious ones: Bonhoeffer, a protestant pastor in Nazi Germany, William Wilberforce, an evangelical Christian in Britain, Desmond Tutu, an Anglican Archbishop in Johannesburg, Oscar Romero a Catholic Archbishop in El Salvador, Mahatma Gandhi, a Hindu in India, and the Dalai Lama, a Buddhist leader in Tibet.

The religions that have nurtured these pioneers, now take pride in being associated with them, though it was not always so. They are the 'saints' that have risen above their religions to show their faith traditions in a better light. They have done so because they have separated the spiritual and the religious strands of faith, and realised that when there is a clash between right and wrong, between good and evil, the strength of their convictions will come from their spiritual integrity, not their religious adherence.

For them spirituality was 'far more than a science of interpreting exceptional private experiences'. Instead, in Archbishop Rowan Williams' definition, it is something that 'must touch every area of human existence, the public and the social, the painful, negative, even psychological byways of the mind, the moral and rational world.' Religion has allowed itself to be compartmentalised by society all too easily, being seen as another source of community interest and activity: a life style choice that corroborates society's current values, but that ultimately knows its place, and does not rock the boat in any serious way.

In contrast, spirituality begins from the premise that there is no area of being and of doing that can be excluded from scrutiny because human beings are not just subjects or citizens. Rather they have infinite capacity to be both magnificent and base, incredibly altruistic and depressingly selfish. Spirituality's gift is that it clarifies the choice that is everyone's to make. The Bonhoeffers and the Tutus, the Wilberforces and the Luther Kings stood out from the faith traditions in which they were nurtured because they drew on faith's substance rather than adhering to its outward form. Their religion taught them about God, their spirituality enabled them to meet with God. It was the meeting, not the doctrine, that was transforming. To see yourself, however fleetingly, as God sees you, is to see others as God must see them.

If 'man is the measure of all things' there is no larger ideal against which to set human achievement and to judge human failure. Whereas, when you have looked into the eyes of God and been aware of God looking into your own eyes, you become aware of your own human potential and that of all human kind in a way that is of quite a different order. There will be elements of shame and regret in any encounter with God, but the dominant experience will be one of enlargement and of affirmation, of growing into one's full humanity. Spirituality exposes the shallowness of the inferior-superior lie of racism.

Scholar and novelist, Davies Aberpennar, wrote one of his most memorable poems about an incident that happened to him and his young grandson when they were out walking in the high street, and they passed a little Asian lad. What transpired between the two boys, one white, one black, was no more than 'a mischievous nod full of unconditional friendship'. But for Davies, it was infinitely more significant:

'The primitive gravity
that would draw awareness to awareness, vivacity to vivacity, body
to body was disclosed.
From the eyes of the one to the eyes of the other
flowed the sacred delight. Between them leapt the joyful electricity
which proclaims
that our humanity is both one and many
that each living soul is unique and common.'

Whatever it was that happened to Peter, James and John, alone with Jesus and God on the mountainside, 'from the eyes of one to the eyes of the other flowed sacred delight'. They too had been transfigured and had seen 'that our humanity is both one and many'. That what had started as 'an exceptional private experience' had ended knowing that their future, Jesus' future, would also have to touch every human experience, not least the painful and the negative.

Racism happens when in fear or uncertainty, or because of insults imagined or received, we retaliate and react with crude assertions of superiority: intellectual, moral, cultural. In Jesus's company his followers learnt not only that where there is love there can be no fear, but that God is love and that they and all humankind were children of God.

Such outworking will always be costly, because to challenge any evil is at a price. It would take Jesus to a Roman cross, and James would be beheaded by the Jewish puppet king. Peter too, and possibly John and most of the twelve, would all have to pay the ultimate price for defying the principalities and powers whose survival depended on hierarchies of subservience.

Spirituality's secret is that each of those sacrifices, which at the time might not register as particularly significant, other than to those who were their nearest and dearest, made a difference to the balance of right and wrong in the human economy. Martin Luther King, who was himself assassinated for his stand against racism, explained it in terms of the redemptive quality of unearned suffering. This is not the language of politics or governance, but it finds a resonance with those who might not know how to put it into words, but who acknowledge that when a good person suffers or dies in a just cause, something bad has been halted in its tracks, if only momentarily. Each little victory for spirituality is a promise that ultimately right will triumph.

There may be something sweetly touching in the Spinners' old lyric:

'A child is black, a child is white
The whole world looks upon the sight
A beautiful sight'

with its subsequent claim:

'And very well the whole world knows
This is the way that freedom grows.'

But the truth is otherwise. What the whole world knows from bitter experience, is that it's not as easy as that. For freedom to grow, it has to be fought for on many fronts. Thus those who have challenged racism have found themselves not only taking on their country's laws, but also their own religion's compliance with those laws.

Bayers Naude and Allan Boesak may be names that are now fast disappearing into the sands of time, but in apartheid South Africa they were highly significant and controversial figures. They spoke out against state sponsored racism as pastors from within the Dutch Reformed Church to which they belonged, a church that was providing an iniquitous regime with its theological legitimacy.

Desmond Tutu belonged to a different church, but shared the same faith and the same struggle. Because of his moral and spiritual stature he ensured that the message was heard around the globe. 'In setting us free to be His children,' the Archbishop proclaimed, 'God wants to enlist us in His service as co-workers with Himself in the business of the Kingdom.' It was Tutu's humanity that enabled him to be heard by those who might not be interested in his religion, but who willingly acknowledged his spirituality. Because all have been created in the image of God, Tutu saw it as our human calling and our glorious destiny 'to labour with God to humanize the universe and to help his children become ever more fully human.'

Even those impervious to the arguments of faith recognise that racism destabilises societies, and that unstable societies affect the peace of the world. The lessons of the Bonhoeffers and the Tutus, the Naudes and the Boesaks is that ultimately the moral force to resist and to undermine racism has to be based on an image in which the human mind is not the measure of all things. Their achievement was also to realise that the struggle against racism invariably involves challenging the premises of nationalism that makes its own claim on religion's allegiance. Racism is nation-alism's handmaid, with religion often becoming handmaid to both. Each is based on a model of exclusion and relies on arguments of superiority.

Nationalism is not the same as nationhood. Nationalism wants conformity and imposes uniformity. Nationhood cherishes diversity and encourages variety. Nationalism is narrow, inward looking and selective. Nationhood is broad, self respecting and inclusive. Nationhood must challenge nationalism if it is to deny racism its unwholesome comfort zone.

The concept of a chosen people is always a dangerous one if it implies status or privilege. The only choice God makes of us is to love our neighbour as ourselves. To vow to our country 'all earthly things above', as in Cecil Spring Rice's hymn, is dangerously jingoistic even with the awareness in his second verse of 'another country' whose 'fortress is a faithful heart, her pride is suffering'. Far nearer to the critical belonging that is the hallmark of nationhood are the poems of that other first world war soldier, Wilfred Owen, for whom patriotism demanded the honesty to expose the futility and waste of war and the blundering of those who led them:

'Red lips are not so red
As the stained stones kissed by the English dead'

Nationalism encourages the belief that God is on our side. It fosters the idea in nations great and small that providence has some special purpose for them, a destiny over and above that of all other peoples which only that nation can fulfil. As such it remains a strong element in the self awareness of the American people and draws on a particular Protestant strand within Christianity. But it's there in most nations, and most religions. It is a dangerous creed because it plays the racist game. It encourages the delusion that one's own worth is based on devaluing the worth of another.

Spirituality's agenda is different. Though it stems from the same roots, spirituality speaks the language of internationalism. It not only values distinctiveness, it extols it. It sees nationhood in terms of equality and diversity. Families, tribes, nations are marks of identity to offer to, rather than to mark us off from, other families, tribes and nations. Caste, class, accent, language, colour – they are the badges of who we are, not to be used as a cause or a crusade, to isolate or persecute the other. Rather they are the opposites in which we become aware of the variety and richness of the whole.

For Joan Puls, it was the belief and the hope of the American Fransiscan Order to which she belonged, comprising as it did Latins, Europeans, North Americans and Indians, 'that cross cultural community was possible, that diverse languages, customs, priorities could be pooled in a community open enough and brave enough to plod and press towards that dream.'

On the mountainside Jesus brought a heady brew of race, nationalism and religion together, and transfigured them. Moses had given the Jews laws that made them a nation. At their best they'd been an inclusive people. When Solomon had dedicated their first temple his prayer had been that it would be a place of sanctuary for all nations. Elijah had bequeathed them a prophetic religious tradition in which right behaviour was more important than ritual or religious observance. Calling God 'Holy' produced an echo to love one's neighbour as oneself. God had given them race: the human race. God had created them all equal, neither Jew nor Gentile, just people:

> 'the black and white and yellow and brown –
> man, the chosen creature,
> the Image, the Icon.'

Jesus had brought all these together in himself. On the hillside with Peter, James and John as his witnesses, he had stood before God between Moses and Elijah, to show that humanity alienated by racism and separated into nations could be reclaimed for a world let down by religion.

The racism of Judea in Jesus' time was not that of black and white or even of Jew and Roman. The gulf between those two was of a different order entirely, of people who know they have no more in common with their current occupiers than they had with the Greeks, the Assyrians and the Babylonians before them. The racism in Judea that mattered, that rankled, was that between Jew and Samaritan. The Samaritans were never going to go away.

They were the offspring of Jews that had survived the exile. When others had been re-located to Babylon, they'd been left behind because they didn't matter, they didn't have the clout to cause trouble, to nurture insurrection or disrupt the administration. They were also needed to maintain the infrastructure of the land under its new owners. Willing or unwilling they were seen as collaborators when the exiles came home. There had also been a fair measure of intermarriage over the intervening years. So the returning exiles accused them of losing their Jewishness and the Samaritans replied they should be glad they'd maintained some sort of co-operation with the invaders so there was a homeland for the exiles to come back to. In a land and a history where mountains mattered, Sinai, Hermon and Tabor, where you got nearer to God than on the plain, the Samaritans felt closer to the God of Abraham on mount Gerizim than on any others favoured by those who'd once been their neighbours. Of such things is racism born.

So Jesus went out of his way to talk with Samaritans. He'd once had a remarkable, unconventional conversation with a Samaritan woman while she was drawing water from a well. His friends later recalled the story he'd told of the Samaritan who'd done a good turn to a Jew. So Jesus was keen to include Samaritan settlements in his mission, not just those of his own people.

Samaritans kept themselves to themselves. They had their own towns and cities, the two communities surviving by having as little to do with each other as possible. So they were not particularly impressed to hear Jesus, a Jew, wanted to share his message with them. Perhaps they'd heard about his preaching and his wonders. What they'd picked up intrigued them, especially the story about a *good* Samaritan. They'd thought that rather telling, especially coming from a Jew! But they didn't know many good Jews, and thought it best to maintain the normal civilities but not start anything that might lead to who knows what. So they'd sent word that a visit from the Jewish Rabbi and his dozen messengers would not be welcome.

For James and John that was a snub too far. They were for cursing the Samaritans out of existence on the spot! Did they hear Jesus's spirit groan at that? Did they see the pain more than the rebuke in his face? Did they notice that upright frame buckle under the weight of some invisible cross? They'd been with him on the mountain. They'd looked into the eyes of God. How could they will the Samaritans into oblivion? Could they not understand the weight of history, the hurts the Samaritans had received at the hands of Jews? That in Samaritan eyes:

'there kindled the flame
of a force which only the black man knows'.

The incident with the Samaritans wasn't the only time James and John had revealed their insecurity. On another occasion they asked for top ranking when Jesus pulled off what they'd expected would be his coup d'etat. Had they heard his spirit groan again? Had they felt his heart sink that their horizons should be so limited, their concepts so nationalistic? Had their understanding of the spirituality they'd shared on the mountain not got beyond that of an exceptional personal experience? Did they not understand that what they had seen and heard had to touch 'every area of human experience, the public, the social, the painful, negative, even psychological byways of the mind, the moral and relational world'?

It was Charles Ward's insight, born of bitter experience and belief, to realise that it's never enough to know the stand you want to make, unless you're also prepared to move in a direction to bring it about. Years later I realise how right he was.

Spirituality alerts us to the reality that racism is not a single evil to be confronted and overcome as part of a more general process of moral improvement. Racism is even more insidious, because it contains within itself all the other ills that separate us from each other and from God: that divide families, that disrupt societies, that drive nations to war. Because spirituality dares to allow us to look into the face of God and have the eyes of God look into our own, the hierarchies of worth are shown to be worthless. It is because we are all equal in the eyes of God that we can do no other than regard and treat everyone else as our equal. It's

'the joyful electricity
which proclaims
that our humanity is both one and many
that each living soul is unique and common.'

III

ALTHOUGH THE ROAD WAS LONG

'Pa hyt bynnac y bydynt ar y ford'

7. Walk in the water:
to belong is to be free

'I was wounded in the house of my friends'

'I go to church ... because I want to ... to fulfil a particular rather than a general need in my life and where I will continue my attachment so long as it provides what I want, but I have no obligation either to attend in the first place or to continue if I don't want to'. The words are Grace Davie's, a sociologist of religion, and they summarise her analysis that the reality for many at the beginning of the twenty first century is 'believing without belonging'. The sacred persists, but not necessarily in traditional forms. Religious membership or practices are at variance with people's stated beliefs. Davie describes this as a shift from an 'ethic of obligation' to an 'ethic of consumption'. And while her conclusions are geared towards the Christian faith, particularly in a Western liberal culture they will also emerge in other faiths eventually, if not so obviously at present.

Religious practice is therefore merely reflecting the attitude we bring to the rest of our social engagement. We have multiple choices at our fingertips from television channels and digital radio stations, to the internet which allows us instant access to information and to contacts, with sites such as 'Facebook', that were previously unimaginable. The global workplace means I can be employed by any country without having to relocate. I may not even need to go out to work every day. I can do most of it from home.

We even have 24/7 shopping and we buy where the price is right or the product is best, not because we've always patronised a certain store or where the proprietor knows us by name. We have the mobility to make and maintain friendships over a wide distance; we are no longer limited to the choices available in our immediate neighbourhood. For millions the world has become in reality as well as in theory our oyster. The changing nature of society coupled with our attitude to time, where for many there is no fixed shape to the week, month, or year, has produced a loose attachment to institutions, including religious ones.

We may have been brought up in such and such a church or in a particular tradition or denomination, or (increasingly) in a specific world faith, but no longer feel tied to it. We go, if we go anywhere, to the place that meets our current needs. Very many have opted to drop out altogether, not necessarily because they have stopped believing, but because they no longer see the point of belonging, or find that belonging has become a hindrance or a switch-off to believing. If we're honest, many of us can sympathise with that view. Because many acts of worship, however well meaning, can be so impersonal or cold, irrelevant or even an insult to our intelligence, it is surprising they continue to attract enough of a congregation to remain in business.

But for how long can a detached spirituality connect with life on anything other than a superficial level? Without some reference points that are earthed in everyday reality and that draw on the experience of others, its adherents, however sincere, become no more than holy dabblers, clutching a ragbag of experiences ranging from the interesting to the downright absurd.

Spirituality is too precious, too real to be allowed to float free from its roots in a faith that is tried and tested. Individuals may differ in their particular take on the various tenets of that faith, but at its core there will be a collective given, a plumb line, against which to test and sift impressions and experiences and to encourage a healthy suspicion of the outlandish.

Creeds, articles of faith, affirmations of belief, mission statements will be of their time, and each and every generation will need to re-interpret them to capture their original relevance and truth. They will always have to be translated from the thought forms and concepts of one culture to another, in the process to become richer, fuller insights into the nature of God, of humankind and of the whole of existence. But it cannot be done in isolation. People do not have to be habitual patrons of a chosen place of worship, but they do need to connect with it in some shape or form however tenuous, because without such a reference point spirituality will unravel into meaningless nonsense or worse.

We cannot, therefore, go on believing in any coherent and satisfying sense without re-engaging with the fundamental importance of belonging as an integral part of believing. My quarrel with some of the advocates of contemporary spirituality is their encouragement of the idea that believing can best flourish when it is uprooted from the soil in which it was nurtured. It's the cult of individualism; it is part of the same mindset that proclaims there is no such thing as society.

But we are social beings. We discover ourselves in relation to others, initially in the family, and then on through school and play and work. 'It is not good for the man to be alone,' God is represented as affirming in one of the oldest creation stories. And it carries a timeless truth about the nature of humankind. We are better together.

It is a mistake Christians make too often to think of Jesus opting out of the Jewish faith in which he was nurtured. He said repeatedly to those who misunderstood his intentions, that his goal was not to destroy the Torah, the Law of Moses, but to live it out. He was faithful in his attendance at synagogue. At his bar mitzvah he deliberately sought out the great religious teachers of his day by slipping away from his family to engage with them for days on end in the great temple in Jerusalem.

Eager eyed and with the little box that cradled words from the Torah still bound tightly to his arm, he'd sat with rapt attention listening as the learned doctors disputed among themselves over the significance of a particular Hebrew letter here or a phrase there, stroking their beards with happy revelation at some new point of law or exegesis. And the youth had joined in, surprising the old hands with the sharpness of his questions and his precocious rhetoric. But that was the way Jews did it. Theirs was not a submissive spirituality. They wrestled with God like their ancestor Jacob at the brook. To argue was to belong.

This is not to suggest that belonging is easy. It isn't. In every context, religious and secular, with family and friends, in and out of work, belonging can test the patience of a saint! It's because we've underplayed the importance and the emotional cost of belonging that we come unstuck when we hit a bad patch. Couples divorce and families break up all too easily when belonging is regarded too lightly.

Jesus fell out with his family, but I don't believe he ever turned his back on them, and at the last his concern was for his mother and her future. He infuriated the congregation in his local synagogue one Sabbath to such an extent that they were ready to lynch him. But he never gave up on them. The prophet Zechariah, who lived and preached in the sixth century BCE, once admitted plaintively, 'I was wounded in the house of my friends'. It's an expression that sums up the cost of belonging. The deepest hurts we experience in life are not inflicted by those we care little for, or who care little for us, but by those we love the most. Jesus was most pained when his own intimate circle let him down.

But this wounding is an integral part of belonging. To belong is to be hurt. Fearing for his life after Jesus's arrest, Peter was challenged outside the court where the trial was being conducted and denied all knowledge of the accused. When Jesus heard of it later the hurt went deep. Peter, whom he'd taken up the mountain and ushered him, with James and John, into the very presence of God, still lacked the confidence in a tight corner to stand by his friend. There had been a lot of bad mouthing over James and John's bid for status too. But it's the hurt, while wounding and often leaving permanent scars, that enables us to grow if we will allow it.

Growth, spiritual as much as any other variety, is painful. And if we think we can avoid it by dropping out or by leaving, we will never mature. Belonging is no defence against being offended, or of offending others. Rather the opposite. It increases our exposure to hurt. But it is as we handle these blows to our self esteem that we grow and relationships deepen. The prophet Isaiah of Babylon was a far more substantial figure than Zechariah. For him the healing, the deep healing, was a shared experience that began when someone else innocently but deliberately took on the wounded party's hurt in order to rob it of its capacity to embitter and to diminish another's life. Believing without belonging can appear an attractive prospect, at least on the surface, but long term it can lead to a shallow, fair weather faith, like the seeds in one of Jesus' stories that never took root or sprouted, and which died when the stones and the weeds got in the way.

The element of belonging is strong in all the World's Faiths. For the Jew, the phrase 'Next year in Jerusalem', said at the end of the Passover Seder, may be anachronistic for a Diaspora that is comfortable and settled in scattered communities throughout the world, but it unites them in their common belonging. It is belonging that underlies the Moslem's obligation to undertake the Hajj, to go on a pilgrimage to Mecca, to walk around the Ka'ba and kiss the black stone in its wall. It is belonging that draws the Hindu to visit the holy city of Benares or to bathe in the river Ganges, or that beckons Confucian, Taoist and Buddhist to visit the graves of their ancestors for the ritual of Ching Ming. It is belonging that makes the Palestinian refugees dream of one day being able to return to their olive groves and lime trees.

In his poem, Sea Fever, John Masefield captures the religious-like pull of particular places or memories, calling us back to what we know, which knows us as we are:

'I must go down to the sea again, for the call of the running tide
Is a wild call and a clear call that may not be denied.'

Few too know the importance of belonging more than those imprisoned and tortured because of their beliefs; the prisoners of conscience who come from all faiths and from none. For them belonging is a life-line not a luxury. It is knowing they are not alone that gives them the strength to endure; knowing that there are people out there who not only refuse to allow them to be forgotten, but who share their fundamental belief in what the historian Christopher Lasch called 'the goodness of life in the face of its limits' which 'cannot be defeated by adversity.'

Even when there exists a degree of religious toleration, believing can still be a balancing act between conflicting expectations. For the Chinese Christian pastor Ma Jian Hua, it's a tight rope she walks daily. In her 40s, Pastor Esther as she's known to her community in Huang Shan City, leads a team of ten lay workers. On a Sunday morning the thousand-seater church she's inspired her people to build against the beauty and grandeur of South Anhui's Yellow Mountain, is full of young people and students as well as of older folk.

There's a quiet intensity and earnestness about this slight, attractive woman that has enabled her not only to survive but to thrive, though it has been at some cost. There were occasions when the local authorities hauled her in for questioning because of something she'd done or said, or been reported to have said or done. His Excellency, Mr Wang Zuo An, the government minister responsible for regulating the five officially recognised faiths in this avowedly atheistic state – Taoism, Confucianism, Buddhism, Catholicism and Protestantism - may have assured the western delegation he was entertaining in a palace in which the last emperor, Pu Yi, had played as a child, that with the end of the cultural revolution and Mao's death in 1976 'people are now allowed to practice their faith openly,' but it was still easy to fall prey to the agendas of petty local officials.

'Everyone needs a personal mark,' Pastor Ma explained as she fingered a finely polished stone seal celebrating the building's anniversary. 'For Westerners, it's a signature, for Chinese it's a seal, and that seal represents the heart of the giver.' Her eyes twinkling with a touching sincerity, she explained, 'Just as no two leaves are the same, no two stones are ever identical. Each is unique.' And for this remarkable, courageous woman whose personal mark was Jesus, it was clearly the belonging that sustained the individual uniqueness. A belonging to God.

A different kind of challenge faced the Chinese layman, Ma Hong Zhi, who worked for the state controlled religious apparatus. Daniel Ma, to give him his Christian name, was based in Shanghai as his church's co-ordinator for overseas relations. His wife had a job in a bank in Nanjing. He saw her, together with their young son, as often as he could. As a government as well as a church employee, Daniel Ma Hong Zhi, like others similarly placed, had to balance his loyalty to his beliefs with his loyalty to the state.

It had been his grandmother's belonging that had nurtured his believing. With the end of the Cultural Revolution the little church in her community had opened its doors once more. Along she went, finding the atmosphere friendly and the message comforting. During the holidays when her little grandson came to stay she took him along too. A generation later Bibles were coming off Amity's presses in Nanjing at the rate of two a minute. Then they were scarce. So one of Hong Zhi's tasks when he stayed with grandma was copying out for her passages of scripture and her favourite hymns, copies of copies more often than not. The experience awakened an interest in the young lad that later led to his being baptised and made a member of China's post denomi-national Protestant church. Meantime he'd graduated in economics and went on to study comparative religions in his spare time. It typifies that blend of ancient culture and Christian faith that Raymond Roselip's haikus capture:

'the firefly you caught
lights the church you make
with your hands'

Daniel's was not an untypical life for an aspiring Chinese citizen. With his mobile phone, smart suit, white shirt and tie, and carrying officially approved handouts, he is part of the new wave that in one generation had made the momentous transition from a rural peasant background to executive class. He's fortunate too in having a job that's compatible with his beliefs; a faith that continues to be nurtured in the local church where he plays an active role. 'It is part of my life,' he explains, 'to help congregations with their spiritual involvement.' So he enrolled for a post graduate course on pastoral ministry, and attended evening classes in psychological counselling.

For this twenty first century Chinese Daniel, his spirituality had been nurtured in and by the local assembly of his co-religionists and it was in and with these people that faith and religion had come together for him. 'Hold a stone and walk in the water,' was one of Daniel Ma's favourite proverbs. 'The only way to maintain your balance when crossing a torrential stream and not to drown,' he expanded, 'was to carry something to provide you with added weight for increased stability.' For this young man, there was no doubt that it was in and with others in the local church that he found the ballast to maintain his balance in a very fast moving secular society.

In contrast, for many, especially in the west, spirituality has become an individual pursuit, something self taught, an amalgam of special moments, of unexplained experiences that have moved them deeply, of things read or seen that have touched chords and lingered in the memory. Even among those who are persuaded that religion and spirituality have a symbiotic relationship, and who are intent on nurturing spiritual growth and development, there are nevertheless some who would still want to distance themselves from belonging in any formal or structural sense.

If believing without belonging is a misnomer, there's another side to belonging, however, that's about breaking free. This is because the best belonging provides the safety and the security to nurture a healthy independence and that gives confidence to develop one's own ideas rather than adopting uncritically the attitudes and outlook handed down by others.

Jesus went to synagogue. As a practising Jew, with his brothers and sisters he looked forward to his mother's Friday meal at the commencement of Shabbat, and to watching their father saying Kiddush. He kept the festivals, asking his people's age old questions at the beginning of Passover. He booed the name of the evil Haman at the party for Purim, lit the menorah at Hanukkah, and prayed for forgiveness and a fresh start at the sound of the shofar, the ram's horn, marking Rosh Hashanah and Yom Kippur at the new year service. But he was also constantly challenging conventional interpretations and practices. 'You have heard it said,' he would interrupt, 'but I say .... ' He encouraged his followers to think for themselves too, to ask awkward questions, especially of those who regarded themselves as infallible!

When Jesus took Peter, James and John up the mount of transfiguration, he showed them how to test the spiritual validity of the voices they were hearing, including even the voice of God. He taught them of the need to set the impressions of their senses against the standards represented by Moses and Elijah. Did they ring true in the light of the legal framework that had given them as a people their identity and purpose? Did the voices they were hearing measure up to the prophetic refrain that cautioned against religious practices that failed to issue in high ethical standards? Did it resonate with Micah's sermon: 'God has told you what is good: and what is it that the Lord asks of you? Only to act justly, to love loyalty, and to walk wisely before your God.'

Before taking Peter and the brothers James and John up the mountain where they saw that splendid sight, Jesus had asked them what they made of him? And there were no marks for pat answers. Peter had no doubt, 'You're God's Chosen' he'd affirmed, but it was some time before he realised the full significance of what he'd said.

In a famous story in the Talmud, the rabbis had been disputing among themselves over the interpretation of a particular scripture. All were agreed on what it meant except for the Rabbi Eliezer, who invoked heaven in defence of his view. Back from above came the apparently confirming reply, 'Why do you dispute the view of Rabbi Eliezer seeing that the law is always in accord with his opinion?' When Rabbi Nathan was later given an audience with Elijah, the traditional go-between in disputes between heaven and earth, he was curious to know how God had reacted to the rest of the rabbis coming to a different conclusion to that of Eliezer, who had, it seemed been endorsed by heaven itself. Had God been tempted to hurl a thunderbolt of disapproval in their direction? Not at all, Elijah explained, rather the opposite. God had laughed, musing approvingly: 'My children have defeated me!'

God is not impressed when we invoke his name to endorse our private opinions. God may play along with them a while, tongue in cheek, but is not deceived. We discern the will of God best when our believing is anchored in our belonging, when our spirituality connects with our religion. Belonging, spiritually as well as in any other sphere of social contact, is not about not disturbing the waters. It's about having the confidence to challenge accepted ways of seeing others and of seeing God, so that the world, the big wide world as well as our own little worlds, can be changed for the better.

It was the belonging that eventually came to Branwen's rescue. After the incident with the horses, which had been patched up with the reparation of replacements and expensive gifts, she'd sailed with her husband to her new home where at first she had been well received and well thought of. But the gossip of the insult traded by her half-brother followed them across the Irish Sea, and slowly public opinion had turned against her, though by then she'd born the king a son and heir. Her fate was to be banished from the royal bed and to suffer a butcher's insults in the royal kitchens as she cooked for the court for ever after. In despair she reared a starling, taught it to speak, then set it free to fly to the Isle of the Mighty to tell her brother, Brân, of her plight. When one type of belonging breaks down, it does not mean the end of all belonging, only that we have recourse to the belonging we know we can trust.

Peter was quite a traditional Jew in many senses. Cut him in half like a piece of seaside rock and you'd find Moses and Elijah written through him from head to toe! For him, non-Jews could only really belong to Jesus' cause if the men accepted circumcision first. It took a particularly vivid dream for him to change his mind and realise that some practices are a hindrance rather than a help to faith. We need to be on our guard against the belonging that cramps rather than releases potential, other people's as well as our own, the belonging that suffocates rather than breathes life into enquiring minds.

When Jesus told a story of two sons, one of whom went off and squandered his share of the family fortune, only to come back with his tail between his legs asking to be re-instated, he was describing a family that had been at logger heads long before the one lad upped sticks and left. The son that stayed at home may have been the solid, dependable kind, but he couldn't for the life of him abide his brother or handle his brother's unconventional life style. The son who left, went because belonging had become a burden, a matter of filial duty.

Among the band of disciples, was Judas's betrayal not so much about Jesus as about the rest of them? Had they belittled him over the years, not taking him seriously? Judas was always an enigma to the eleven. Idealistic, brooding, passionate. Maybe he was always a loner. Perhaps he never fitted in. Jesus believed in Judas, but Judas found it difficult to believe in himself. Had Jesus asked him to look after their finances in order to build up his confidence? We'll never know. But the existence of Judas serves as a warning against idealising relations among the twelve. Belonging is never easy, but without it believing is no more than a private passion.

All the great advances in human understanding and knowledge have been made by people willing to think outside the box, who've challenged the conventional wisdom, who've dared to suggest that the earth goes round the sun, not the other way round, that iron boats can float and ships can take to the air, that living hearts and kidneys can be grafted in to replace faulty organs, that dissonance can create a new kind of harmony. Believing without belonging is a dead end, but belonging always needs to allow for the need for all of us at one time or another to break free. How then are we to hold these two together in some kind of creative tension? Certainly not by denying them. Religious communities have been too ready to promote conformity at the expense of sincerity.

Conformity often means dull adherence to the norms and conventions, the prejudices and prevailing winds, the shibboleths and blind spots of the group. Whereas commitment demands caring about the others in the group, and those outside the group, in a way that allows and encourages them to think the unthinkable and to speak it out loud. When Jesus was no longer with them, the gospel attributed to John would remind them how he'd said, 'I also own other sheep, who don't belong to this sheep pen'. It was a reminder that the best belonging is always open, inclusive, not exclusive.

After the end of the 1914-18 War the Quakers had earned the respect of the Polish community with their quiet efficient distribution of food and clothing in many of the country's villages. When one of them died suddenly from typhus, the villagers with whom he had formed a particularly close bond were in a quandary over where to bury their much loved friend. The only cemetery was that of the Roman Catholic Church, and, as a Quaker, he didn't qualify for internment in consecrated ground. So they did the next best thing and buried him in a grave they'd dug just outside the cemetery's fence. The next morning the authorities discovered that in the night the villagers had moved the fence so that it embraced the grave.

It's a tale that describes the breadth of belonging, and the unqualified response of those who know intuitively that believing implies belonging. Believing without belonging, in Grace Davie's phrase, may be the mark of the present age. There may be some merit to it in some respects. But ultimately, belonging encircles believing, because believing is not about holding to a set of propositions, but about trust in God, a God for whom belonging was and always will be unconditional and unlimited.

Long after that event in the mountains above the garrison town of Caesarea Philippi, where Jesus and the three disciples seemed to have crossed from one reality to another and back again, and to be a changed and chastened team in the process, a little band of believers in Rome found a letter that bore all the hall marks of Peter's preaching. It was a letter in which he described Jesus' followers in collective terms, as a nation, as a race; in which he took it for granted that while their spirituality would have a uniquely personal edge, it could only be honed and refined through the give and take of belonging with others, as he'd once belonged to the twelve.

Peter's own nation had successively lost its sovereignty to Persians and Babylonians, Seleucids and Romans, and was to experience an even worse fate under the emperor Titus when his people would lose their statehood completely. But they never lost their identity, even in the worst of times. They never ceased to belong to each other: as a diaspora, in exile, or as expats. And that's how Peter saw Jesus' new community. They were people whose spirituality shared a common heritage and history.

From the time a Galilean's shadow had first fallen across his nets as he cleaned his boat and counted his catch, to his final captivity in a Roman cell on a capital charge, it was this sense of belonging that had kept Peter going. At first belonging to his family and to his synagogue, then as one of the Twelve. And in Jesus' company Peter had understood how he belonged to God because he belonged to the people of God, how he belonged in particular in order to belong to all of God's creation. 'There was a time when you were nobody special,' he told the small cluster of believers in the empire's capital,' but now you're God's friends. In those days you were no-hopers, but now that God's befriended you, you've got a reason for living.'

But could that include those who called God by another name?

8. A freckled world:
how ecumenical is God?

'Glory to God for dappled things'

What was I doing? A Christian minister addressing an Islamic congregation in a Syrian mosque on the occasion of Friday prayers, and saying, 'Christians and Moslems have much in common'. Had my ecumenism run away with me? Did I no longer believe in the uniqueness of the faith in which I was nurtured and to which I'd been ordained? An ecumenism that spanned the Christian traditions, that sought to find common ground between Catholic and Protestant, that built bridges between Eastern and Oriental Orthodox, and that shaped local partnerships between Anglicans and Baptists was one thing. But an ecumenism that embraced different world faiths was a very different matter. Was it even desirable, let alone possible?

In accepting the invitation to be the main Friday Sermon speaker alongside Sheikh Salah Eddin Kuftaro, in the huge Abu Nour mosque in Damascus I was agreeing, certainly tacitly, that points of contact between world faiths are at least as, if not more, important than those between separate strands of the same faith. As my distinguished host led me into the crowded mosque with its capacity for a congregation of ten thousand, I suddenly felt very small and uncertain. This was a higher profile encounter than I'd anticipated with my words to be translated and broadcast on local television and radio. Was I taking a step too far? Was I compromising my own integrity? Would it be enough to acknowledge, as I would, that as Christians we had an understanding of the role of Jesus in salvation that Moslems didn't share? Would what I had prepared meet the expectation of the occasion, which included a Catholic bishop and members of the core diplomatic?

The Abou Nour mosque was founded in the early part of the twentieth century at the foot of the Kaasyoun Mountain. Expanded into an Islamic Centre on nine floors, it now included three Islamic colleges, two Sharia institutes, an extensive library, dormitories, a refectory and a charity supporting a thousand orphans as well as a mosque. The inspiration of my host's father, the former Grand Mufti of Syria, Sheikh Salah Ahmad Kuftaro, who taught his people that 'we are not Muslims unless we are Christians as well', the institute aims to promote harmony among Muslims, Christians and people of all religions. In front of me and seeming to stretch to infinity on the red and grey medallioned carpet was a sea of men and boys, alarmingly attentive, earnest, certain even, some curious, some suspicious, in traditional white caps and kufi hats, long coats and baggy trousers. In the galleries above, behind the glass screens, were the shadowy faces of scores of faithful Muslim women. 'I speak to you in the name of the loving God, immortal, invisible, God only wise,' I began.

Later, I reflected that within the Christian family it had taken a very long time for its different branches to acknowledge a common ancestry, and that there is still a sense that 'our' lot has a better grasp of the family story that yours. Even where there is this acknowledgement, there is still for some a sense of distance when it comes to accepting the other unconditionally, completely. But it has been one of the great stories of the second half of the twentieth century to see the Christian family, sometimes enthusiastically, sometimes haltingly, reconnecting and discovering, like adopted children, brothers and sisters they never knew they had. As the world has shrunk, as we've travelled more, as we've watched our communities become more cosmopolitan we've also been made to think about our relationships with and our understanding of those who have a different view of God.

For some, in every world faith, the issue is clear. Whatever these others say, whatever they think, they are wrong. In their ignorance they may believe they are talking to and about God as 'we' know God, but they are deluded and it is our duty, if we care about truth and the eternal salvation of others, to disabuse them, to point out the error of their way, and to integrate them into the one and only faith, which is 'ours'. Any accommodation with other world faiths however well meaning is syncretism.

In 1991 I remember being both electrified and perturbed when Dr Chung Hyung Kyung, a young Korean feminist theologian, invoked the spirits of 'earth, water and sea creature' in a dramatic presentation on the theme of the Holy Spirit and the renewal of creation at a churches assembly in Canberra. In her diaphanous white robe, accompanied by Australian aborigines in loin cloths and body paint, she set alight a rice-paper scroll recording the names of women and men from Hagar to Jesus who had been the victims of oppression. And as the ashes took to the air she drew parallels between the Christian understanding of the Holy Spirit and the Korean goddess of compassion and wisdom, Kwan In, who delays her passage to nirvana to help others achieve enlightenment.

It was a highly contentious if courageous presentation that received a well deserved standing ovation from many of the three and a half thousand in the audience and from those watching on closed circuit television, but it almost resulted in an irrevocable split between the traditional and the liberal wings of the Christian world family. I found myself applauding Dr Chung's desire to commend Christian spirituality to her own Korean culture by making such an imaginative theological leap, and by implication urging others to be equally bold in theirs, but I was unconvinced that this really was the way forward for inter-faith dialogue.

It was all a far cry from my background in west Wales where time stood still. Korea was a country to which we sent missionaries. Even within the Christian world view we were choosy. First and foremost we were Protestants. Roman Catholics barely registered on our radar, though I had a Calvinistic Methodist aunt who was sent to a Catholic school for reasons I could never fathom. Confession seemed too easy an option compared with making the most of one's guilt. And if we were 'Prots' first and last, then being Nonconformist, or 'Free Church' as gentility renamed us later - ran it a close second. The Anglicans were neither one thing nor the other, though my father had a soft spot for them, which we put down to his years in the army! Then I went to Oxford which is a very Anglican University, and all that nonconformity came apart!

Christian ecumenism is still not to everyone's taste, and every act of union seems to be frustrated by further fractures as the champions of the unchanging truth declare their unilateral independence. It is as if we cannot handle the concept of being true to ourselves and accepting, without wanting to change the authenticity of others. 'Ecumenical conversation is not an exercise in diplomacy;' the distinguished Church historian, Henry Chadwick once proclaimed, 'once we think of it in that way we think that, if anything actually moves in this deadlock, this is because someone has made a concession, has compromised with principles, has watered down the truth. This is a disastrous illusion. True ecumenism is not diplomacy: it is kneeling and listening, in the presence of God, with brothers and sisters in Christ from whom the accidents of history have divided us, and asking God how we may learn from one another.'

We have undoubtedly learned from one another to such an extent that Christian ecumenism is now a given. We may still not yet be able to hear this rich diversity in all its harmony, but most expressions of the church no longer anathematise the other. Some may still regard others as flawed or less than the best, but only the most extreme question that all now share the same DNA.

Harmony perhaps is the wrong word to describe this way of hearing different voices and of holding them together in some kind of creative tension. Dissonance might be nearer the mark; the sound made by untrained voices singing the same notes together, some straining and sharpening the pitch, others missing and flattening it, resulting in a cluster of quarter tones rather than a shared note. It's a practice particularly associated with Charles Ives, the innovative American Composer. Ives reproduced in the concert hall what he heard in the street. He composed music in which he depicted competing brass bands passing each other, and in the distance music coming from nearby cafes, and gospel songs from mission halls, intermingling them to make a disturbingly honest picture in sound. Ives wasn't particularly interested in whether his audiences liked what they heard. If they found it shocking or distasteful, that was because society had become complacent. Ives did what he felt he had to do, which was to face them with an uncomfortable truth.

The process of churches coming closer together also involves facing uncomfortable truths about ourselves and about others. If we find these truths shocking or distasteful it is because we have become uncritically satisfied with our own church or denomination with little appetite to enquire into the spiritual reality of other churches and denominations.

All such processes of enquiry produce tensions that can lead to further frustrations, but, sad as that might be, there will be no reversing the conviction that whatever the inadequacies - in our eyes - of the other, God intends that we belong together. We shall still have to do battle with the perception that compromise challenges conviction, that our convictions oblige us to set acceptable limits to our diversity. But why do we need to start from here? Setting limits, however generous, implies that before embarking on the quest we are unwilling to follow it through regardless of the discoveries we may make about ourselves and others on the way. It betrays an attitude in which subconsciously 'our' truth is the whole truth, come what may, and while there may be room to view 'our' truth from fresh angles, it will be the same truth as we have always held it to be.

Setting limits is the language of religion. Religion fears uncertainty. If we do not say 'so far and no further' we will be lost. This is because our point of reference is a proposition rather than a relationship. Would not a better place to begin be with the pursuit of diversity, which is the language of spirituality? And is this not nearer to the nature of the God whose character permeates all living things?

It is captured in the taut but perceptive 'Pied Beauty' of Gerald Manley Hopkins' poem of glory to God:

> 'Whatever is fickle, freckled (who knows how?)
> With swift, slow; sweet, sour; adazzle, dim;
> He fathers-forth whose beauty is past change.'

The natural order survives and develops because of diversity. Species survive because they adapt. And the species that become extinct are those that have failed to evolve. Civilisations rise and fall according to their capacity to accommodate themselves to changing circumstances. The Christian 'take' on God as a 'trinity', taxes the comprehension of the literal minded. We should understand the Trinity as a marker placed against the idea of a monochrome God. The diversity of the cosmos indicates a personality and a mind, behind and within it, that is fascinatingly, attractively, richly dappled. 'In the third millennium many possibilities exist for bringing the various religious traditions into a positive and mutually enriching relationship', Oxford academic, Keith Ward reminds us. 'For that to happen, the traditions must not be destroyed, but must remain as witnesses to the diversity of human understanding of God, a diversity which will remain within any wider convergence of traditions.'

When Martin Luther famously declared: 'Here I stand, I can do no other', having posted his 95 theses to the doors of the church in Wittenberg, was he just setting limits or doing something much more significant? We have commonly seen Luther's theses as a call to first principles and to a rooting out of ecclesiastical corruption.

And it was that. But it was also a call to his church to adapt to a changing world whilst being, and in order to be, true to itself and its message. The concept of a united Europe, under the acknowledged sovereignty of Emperor or Pope, was giving way to the reality of nation states. Printing would make new ideas accessible to a mass market. The Renaissance was consigning closed minds to the sidelines of history. If the church was to have a message relevant to this changing world, it would need to recognise these changes and find ways of telling the old, old story in a way that people would see its contemporary relevance as well as its eternal value.

The significance of the juxtaposition of Jesus with Moses and Elijah on the mount of transfiguration was its endorsement of Jesus as part of the continuity represented by the Torah, alongside the prophetic tradition, which at its best challenged succeeding generations to re-think their faith. For Elijah, who served Yahweh, each country had its peculiar and distinct god or gods. The God of Israel might be of a better kind than neighbouring gods, demanding higher moral values than the Syrian Rimmon, but deity was still an unrefined concept. It took the experience of exile in a foreign land for the Jews to re-think their beliefs and to formulate a theology of the one universal God. In the process they would also be driven to re-visit their concept of individual responsibility. The corporate calamity of exile required acceptance of personal failure too. Each individual had contributed to shaping and deciding the destiny of their nation. Changing circumstances required them to formulate a theology that was both universal and particular.

Why then do we find the idea of re-thinking our beliefs in the light of changing experience so alien when our history, the history of the world, abounds with examples of seeing God differently because we stand in a different place from those who went before us? When John Mortimer entitled his affectionate on-stage autobiography, 'Voyage round my father', he tapped into a universal if not always acknowledged experience, namely that how we see the other differs with the passage of time. As he grew up, Mortimer saw his blind, eccentric but hugely influential barrister father in a new light. His father was the same father he'd always been, but it was a voyage of discovery in which the familiar was revealed through unfamiliar insights. It's a journey, a progressive revelation, and it is only when we avoid, or become unwilling to embark on such voyages that we become blasé about what life can offer.

On the mountain, Peter, James and John were given their clearest insight yet into the kind of person Jesus was. Here was no ordinary rabbi. How extraordinary he was they were not to fathom for some time to come. On the way, together with Philip, Thomas, Judas and the rest, they would learn by means of a succession of eye-opening experiences. When Jesus took on the religious leaders of his day, it was not to belittle them, but to challenge them to re-think what they meant by God, a God for whom Samaritans were as precious as Jews, who had time for the distraught parents of sick children, and for Roman occupiers.

The essence of life lies in our capacity to be open to change, to see what's good in what's new, and to take that into our system. In the process we too will undergo a degree of change, and those we encounter may also be changed by meeting us. But the change will not be random. It will be with reference to our core beliefs. It will be refining, enlarging, enriching, but never denying. We live in a time of unprecedented change. My great grandparents would have shared a world view with their forebears going back countless generations. My world view on the other hand is so radically different from theirs because of advances in science, medicine, psychology and the arts, that they would be bewildered by a lifestyle that I take for granted, however critically.

In this bluster of change, without always realising it, we have become frightened that we might lose our way. We might no longer know who we are or where we're going. So we set ourselves false limits and boundaries, which only add to our uncertainties. Already, a century and a half ago, change was being associated with decay, and a hymn by the Anglican clergyman Henry Francis Lyte: 'Abide with me', popular for Royal weddings, will still be sung today despite its ominous reflection: 'change and decay in all around I see'. But it's a false comparison, because change as often as not brings life, hope, surprise.

Too often we have used religion to mark out these self imposed limits and made religion an obstacle to progress, an inhibiting, prohibiting framework that holds us back and feeds our guilt. If religion is to be re-instated as the force for good it should be, it will need to be unharnessed from these cautious restraints. It will need to rediscover the venturesome element that is of the essence of spirituality. Religions clash, as do traditions within religions, because they are based on the reassurance of an unchanging continuity. But there is no such thing, except in the field of cloning, which spells disaster for any species. We will only ever make progress spiritually and humanly if we approach the being of God from the angle of where we are now, not where others before us or elsewhere in the world say we should be.

Michael Taylor, emeritus professor of social theology in Birmingham University, once proposed that the only way forward for ecumenism was to see the goal less in terms of pursuing unity in agreement, as forging communities of disagreement 'where being together and being at odds are not seen as mutually exclusive but equally necessary.' And, perhaps, in terms of structural association that might be the only realistic way forward. But in terms of being open to the infinite possibilities of diversity, do we not need to discover how it is possible to be different together?

There is, of course, a significant variation between overcoming the hostility and the bitterness that have marred relationships within a single religion, and in some cases still do, where the history and the core are shared, even if the interpretation and the outworking are disputed, and of overcoming suspicion of different religions. There have been concerted efforts in recent years to trace the common ground between the three faiths that look to Abraham as their common source, namely Judaism, Christianity and Islam. These faiths proclaim one God, have definitive written sources, and interpret creation as a time-line with a definite beginning and end. But what of Hinduism and Buddhism, which see creation in cyclical terms? Can we ever expect to make common cause over such diversity?

The answer will depend on how we see God. If God is created in our own image, then the task had best be not begun. But if we hold that we are created in the image of God, then we can do no other than seek God in the other. At the same time as Lyte was bewailing the decay that he saw coming in the wake of change, the Congregationalist Leeds solicitor, George Rawson could take the opposite view, averring:

> 'We limit not the truth of God
> To our poor reach of mind,
> By notions of our day and sect,
> Crude, partial and refined'

That approach spells the best hope for inter-religious dialogue. But let's not deceive ourselves that it will be any easier than the ecumenism of one faith. If anything it will be more difficult with the cries of compromise, betrayal and syncretism rising on all sides. 'Christians and Moslems must join hands to ensure that religion, like fire or water, is always a force for good in the world,' I appealed in my address to the Abu Nour congregation in Damascus, 'not one that causes hatred or leads to war.'

Overlooking Willen Lake in Milton Keynes stands the Buddhist Peace Pagoda and Temple of the Japanese Nipponzan Myohoji monastic order. It is now an established feature in the life of that remarkable and innovative city. But a quarter of a century ago, when it was very new, I was criticised by some of the more conservative elements within the city's Christian community for offering public prayer at an inter-faith service at the Pagoda. In one sense I could sympathise with their concerns, because I came from a similar background. The criticisms were more painful, since those who spoke them were 'my' people. It was nevertheless another beginning to the voyage round my God.

Whether or not he intended it in a religious sense, or his readers understood it as such, when William Wordsworth's wrote of the child being father of the man in his Ode on Intimations of Immortality from Recollections of Early Childhood, he was drawing on an insight with unmistakeable Buddhist resonances:

> 'Our birth is but a sleep and a forgetting;
> The Soul that rises with us, our life's Star,
> Hath had elsewhere its setting,
> And cometh from afar;
> Not in entire forgetfulness,
> And not in utter nakedness,
> But trailing clouds of glory do we come
> From God, who is our home.'

Martin Palmer, the General Secretary of the Alliance of Religions and Conservation, whose work involves him in supporting and building a Buddhist monastery in Mongolia, restoring forests in India sacred to Lord Jugganath, and preserving Taoist mountains in China, finds himself often having to explain, 'Yet I am also a Christian'. For him, the yin and yang of Taoism has provided release from what he describes as 'the terrible idea that one view is Right and the other Wrong. They just are. It is the use to which their distinctive elements are put that makes for right and wrong.'

Jesus' harshest words were for those who did not live up to the moral imperatives of their faith. Many were more concerned with religious observance than with the kind of down to earth spirituality that takes care of a mugged victim on the road between Jerusalem and Jericho. The world of other faiths is not based on testing the degree to which the other's faith measures up to or matches ours, and proceeding on the basis of some percentage pass mark. Rather it is about realising how often our world views match, and marvelling at their similarity from such apparently different sources.

Scientific discoveries, travel, and huge population shifts in recent time have led us to describing our planet as a global village. It is a situation that is both exciting and dangerous. We can either find a way of living at peace with each other, within communities and between countries, or we can revert to a primeval chaos in a pointless clash of civilizations. Since people define themselves in terms of their religion, it matters that the dialogue between people is also a dialogue between faiths, which is likely to be most productive as a dialogue that sees spirituality as the common thread.

When, in response to the message of the little starling, Brân brought his armies to rescue his sister Branwen from her life of misery in the kitchens of the Irish court, they first had to cross the river Liffey. With the bridges destroyed to impede their progress, and the waters unsafe because of the loadstone on its river bed to suck them under, they found themselves stranded. Brân, however, was as tall as he was brave, and in the moment of crisis, when retreat rather than victory seemed their only option, he became himself the bridge over which his men could cross. Ever after on the Isle of the Mighty it was passed down from one generation to another that 'he who would be a leader must also be a bridge'. Where religions clash because it is of their nature to preserve what makes them distinctive, it is spirituality's gift to provide a bridge that enables faith to speak peace to faith. Spirituality is more concerned with what religions have in common than in what keeps them apart. 'Spirituality liberates us from our religious ghettoes', the Hindu monk and Delhi social activist, Swami

Agnivesh teaches. 'It dismantles barriers and enables inter-religious partnerships. This is basic to the liberation that spirituality affords.'

Little bridges are therefore built every time people of different faiths meet in homes and halls to share their life experiences, listening to the other's scriptures and hearing the resonances in their own. Bridges that may sometimes sway alarmingly in the wind, but that somehow don't give way. Bridges that connect separate banks, enabling the crossing of one to the other; bridges that are built when people of faith are invited to share in each other's feasts and discover the spirituality that informs and sustains those whose name for God is different from their own. Where confidence abounds, honesty is possible.

But what of the bridge between this world and the next? Is that religion's last stand, and spirituality's lie?

9. Hereafter:

beyond both religion and spirituality

'Though lovers be lost love shall not'

'Religion was a lie that he had recognised early in life and he found all religions offensive, considered their folderol meaningless, childish, couldn't stand the complete unadultness – the baby talk and the righteousness and the sheep.' Philip Roth, America's distinguished novelist and man of letters is describing a seventy-one year old Jewish roué facing his physical deterioration and approaching death without the aid of religion or philosophy. In one sense the novel, 'Everyman', echoes Dylan Thomas's poem to his dying father: 'Do not go gentle into that good night' with its defiant imperatives:

> *'Old age should burn and rave at close of day;*
> *Rage, rage against the dying of the light.'*

but Thomas seems to keep the door open to something beyond, to some sense of immortality, especially in his poem, 'And death shall have no dominion,' with its expectation that:

> *'They shall have stars at elbow and foot;*
> *Though they go mad they shall be sane,*
> *Though they sink through the sea they shall rise again;*
> *Though lovers be lost love shall not.'*

Roth's is a much bleaker prognosis. 'There's no remaking reality. Just take it as it comes,' is this anti-hero's attitude to life; and it's something his daughter, Nancy, repeats over his grave: 'Hold your ground and take it as it comes. There's no other way.' It is a very down to earth philosophy and one that chimes in with Western liberal thought at the beginning of the twenty-first century. Not just secular Jew, but secular everyone. Belief in life after death is a shaky proposition for broad swathes of the thinking public. Surveys may indicate a residual reluctance to give up on it entirely, but essentially it is often no more than a consolation, a hoping against hope. In his poignant elegy for his parents, both now dead, Tony Harrison can't quite let go:

'I believe life ends with death, and that is all.
You haven't both gone shopping; just the same,
In my new black leather phone book there's your name
And the disconnected number I still call.'

Like Harrison many can no longer latch onto the reasoning that gives credibility to life after death. We have lost the intellectual framework in which survival beyond the grave is not just a nice possibility but the inevitable consequence of belief in a God of love. For Christians this has to do with the resurrection of Jesus. For Buddhists it is through reincarnation, which is not an endless recycling to a higher or lower life form in a wholly temporal existence, but a progressive refinement until the soul achieves Nirvana, and is at one with all that is. The pyramids of the Egyptian Pharaohs, the terracotta army of the first Qin emperor, the Greek myth of the River Styx, separating this world from the next, are all echoes of a time when a belief in life after death, if only for the privileged, was not inconsistent with advanced cultures.

'There's no other way,' says Roth's anti-hero. 'Just take it as it comes.' Faced with what life can and often does bring, there's a form of relief in accepting the inevitable. Yet for many in the world the inevitable can be desperately awful. It's a philosophy that, even in the worst of circumstances, belittles the potential of what it is to be human. For those with more say over their lives, it denies the effects of the choices they've made. Can a realistic spirituality not allow us the best of both worlds, of keeping the door open to something more without having to explain or justify it, whilst yet remaining rooted in the here and now, since 'nothing is real which is not earthed'?

In a rational existence, where overtones of spirituality persist, what's the point of heaven? 'Thy will be done on earth,' was the pattern of prayer Jesus gave to his disciples. On earth, that's where life has to be lived out. Fantasising about the hereafter is at best an indulgence, at worst a massive distraction, a get-out from the business of making sense and making better the lives and loves we have. In times gone by it was easier to see the point of heaven and of hell. It was a powerful ethical motivator. What you did here and now would affect where you ended up in the hereafter. Good behaviour put you on track for heaven. For bad behaviour, it wasn't just the denial of heaven, or merciful nothingness, but endless, eternal torture.

The frescoes and wall paintings in churches across the world depict the prospect of getting it wrong in grisly detail, and in literature, Dante's Divine Comedy is no joke but a forensic analysis of the failures of his time and the price to be paid. Milton's Paradise is Lost and not lightly Regained. The message is unambiguous: Watch what you do, for lo your sins will find you out, and the consequences are dire. Implicit too was the recognition that however far short one may have fallen, there was always hope that the worst consequences could be avoided by true contrition, repentance, and the intention to reform. Nevertheless Christian theology, building on its Jewish roots, reminded sinners that there was still a price to pay for forgiveness to be granted and received: a goat to be driven out to perish in the wilderness, a man to die on a cross. Humanity was both the cause of its own downfall and ultimately its salvation, till, in Milton's thought,

'one greater Man
Restore us, and regain the blissful seat'.

This whole business of right living was a serious enterprise, and someone had to settle the score when it went wrong. It was as well that people didn't forget it.

The story of Branwen in the Celtic folk tale of the Mabinogion is not ultimately about a beautiful princess from the Isle of the Mighty who became Queen of Ireland and fell from grace, but about her brother and her half brother. They are the characters and personalities that intrigue and puzzle us. They are the ones in whom we see reflected the choices that also face us. At the end both brothers die, both performing unselfish acts, but the outcome in each case is dramatically different because their knowledge of themselves and their view on life is so radically different.

Efnysien has spent his life fighting his demons and is ultimately overcome by them. He has never been able to face the reality of who he is or of those around him, or of his sister's marriage and the birth of her son. He has maimed the horses of the king who wed her, and finally killed the boy, Gwern, heir to the joint kingdoms of Britain and Ireland, in an act of jealous rage.

In a final showdown with his demons, overcome by remorse at the loss of life for which he's been responsible, Efnysien performs one last act that is against his own self-interest. He destroys the Cauldron of Rebirth which revived the enemy dead, which in turn led to his losing his own life. At the end of an almost totally nihilistic life, Efnysien seems to be doing something for others, but it is un-thought through, and ultimately self defeating, since 'There was no real victory, except that seven men escaped.'

Brân, on the other hand, seeing his army is defeated, gives his life that Branwen may live. He orders his companions to cut off his head that it might become a talisman to protect them from the pursuits of their enemy while they lead his sister back to safety on the Isle of the Mighty. His sacrifice assures her survival, and at the end of all their exploits and their collective loss of memory the seven loyal companions fulfil his final wish and take his head to London, where they bury it as he had directed on the White Mount. How we die is directed by how we live, which is what this tale is about. Faith though is concerned with a different time span.

When Michelangelo painted The Last Judgement on the wall of the Sistine Chapel in Rome, he created not only an artistic but a theological masterpiece. Adam, the supreme achievement of creation, brought into existence by the very finger of God, had failed, but could yet fulfil his destiny in, and for all eternity. So the centrepiece of that heaving mass of ethereal and earthly beings is not God but humanity, the sinner saved, because that was the divine plan from the dawn of time.

If it was easier to see the point of heaven and of hell in a previous age as an incentive to a more moral life, it was also easier to understand its attraction in terms of justice. The inequalities of life on earth would be redressed in the hereafter. Those who seemed to have got away with murder in this life would get their comeuppance in the next. And those wronged on earth would be recompensed in the next. The Jewish narrative, Job, is a powerful argument for the reversal of fortunes for the person who remains faithful to principles and to God. In that case the reversal takes place in this life, but the message is transferrable to the world to come: 'in my heart I know that my vindicator lives.'

Jesus' story of Dives and Lazarus, or Desmond, the wealthy man who ignored the plight of Larry, a homeless soul, and ended up in hell, in the re-worded Good as New version, places the action firmly beyond the grave. In the 'miserable and hopeless place' in which Desmond finds himself, he has a moment of altruism and asks permission to return to earth to warn his kin of what will befall them too if they don't mend their ways and look out for the unfortunates on the edges of their existence. But the request is denied by the revered patriarch Abraham, with the implication that we have all the moral imperatives we need to lead decent, caring lives without supernatural intervention. 'Remember, my boy, when you were alive, you had it good,' is Abraham's verdict, 'whereas Larry had a rough time of it. He's having a good time now and you're suffering.' Nowhere has the doctrine of the reversal of fortune been more poignantly repeated and recorded than in the spirituals of the slaves who appropriated the theology which their white owners had chosen to ignore:

'Wish I's in heaven settin' down, settin' down
O Mary
O Martha
Wish I's to heaven settin' down
Wouldn't get tired no mo', tired no mo'
Wouldn't get tired no mo'
O Mary
O Martha
Wouldn't get tired no mo'
Wouldn't have nothing to do, nothing to do
Wouldn't have nothing to do
O Mary
O Martha
Wouldn't have nothing to do.'

Heaven and hell have therefore played a formative part in the moral development of society and its basis in natural justice. But we no longer think that way. That was then. This is now. Our morality may be every bit as high as in a bygone age, in some cases higher (as with an aversion to all forms of torture, and a condemnation of capital punishment), but we no longer see the need for it to be underpinned by a theology. Our morality is sustained and refined by humanism. Rational beings treat each other humanely and decently, and where they don't there are non barbaric but none the less stringent procedures and sanctions to be brought into play based on the ultimate nobility of every person. In a post-theological age the point of heaven as a moral incentive and a corrective to incomplete justice loses its force. Rather we need to see the point of the hereafter providing a different perspective on life now because the here and now is incomplete without it. Maybe we have been too cavalier in dismissing the possibility of eternity as something that belonged to a less sophisticated period, forgetting its role as a counter-weight that held everything else in balance.

Roth called his tale 'Everyman' in a deliberate allusion to the mediaeval morality plays that recounted the story of existence from creation to the last judgement in scenes enacted by travelling players on the back of farm carts in town squares. It was a cautionary tale of paradise lost and regained, of heaven as everyone's destiny and hell as its antithesis. For Roth's 'everyman', however, there is no grand design to life, just taking it as it comes; pointless, foolish, fatuous. It is very much twenty-first century 'everyman', certainly liberal, Western 'everyman'. Roth's antihero may be no more hedonistic than many, but beyond the progression from youth to a career and the pursuit and loss of numerous relationships, there's an unmistakeable despair. He cannot see a meaning to his existence beyond holding his ground. He has no philosophy or spirituality with which to answer the question: what is the point of life?

Roth's anti-hero recognises the need for forgiveness for having wronged the women he's loved and lusted after, and for having alienated the sons of his first marriage. But he can only hope to be pardoned posthumously by those still living. From his daughter, Nancy, he does get forgiveness, but it's not been able to change his perspective on his own life and his estimation of other people's worth. This 'everyman' is literally hope-less. A generation that recognises itself to a greater or lesser extent in this nameless 'everyman', is going to have to find out how to think its way from an everyman who lives in the middle of nothingness to the 'everyman' who sees him and herself as an integral part of something bigger. Someone who does not deny the enlightenment, who is not afraid to be rational, but who also recognises and embraces the non-rational element of his or her being.

Whatever happened on the mountainside above Caesarea Philippi two thousand years ago, it gave Peter, James and John and their successors a world view that had, and still has lasting repercussions that shook the Roman Empire and outlived it, and generated ideas and movements that challenged the lives and destinies of endless generations to come. At its core was this unreasonable reasonable belief not just in a god, in a first principle, but in one whose essence was love, intangible but defining love, whose creative energy conceived humankind and courted a lasting partnership with it. If all this seems too limited, too narrow for an 'everyman' who knows that the stars are not windows into the heaven of a three tiered universe, but balls of fire millions of light years away, many of which have already burnt themselves out by the time their traces appear in our firmament, each with its own planetary systems, then we need to think again. Because there was and is more to God than Peter, James and John were able to conceive of then or any of their successors since, and it is only the self imposed limitation of our own imaginations that catches us out and prevents us from being dazzled by the glory of who we can be because of who He is. So Sydney Carter wonders how 'every star shall sing a carol', posing the question:

'Who can tell what other cradle?
High above the Milky Way;
Still may rock the King of Heaven
On another Christmas day.
Who can count how many crosses?
Still to come or long ago
Crucify the King of Heaven ... '

On the mountainside Peter, James and John entered into the mind and heart of God, but their grasp of God was relative to their capacity and experience. Jesus' knowledge of the world, and theirs will have been as limited to their time as ours is to ours. But they will have experienced God with an intensity and a clarity that is still, and will be while life lasts, everyone's heritage. 'We were not following a cleverly written-up story when we told you about the power and coming' of Jesus, 'we actually saw his majesty with our own eyes.'

I have stood at many gravesides and in front of crematoria catafalques reminding mourners that their loved ones are not in those florally decorated wooden boxes or wicker baskets. Each time it has been a costly exercise, especially when the life recalled has been that of a baby, a child or a young person. In the private place of thought and prayer, the intellectual validity behind the liturgical and pastoral formularies have had to be fought over and wrested from the pull of a culture that knows how to be sentimental but not what it believes. As a child of my time I understand what it is to be agnostic, but I also have a parallel intellectual framework that I believe to be more reliable. But each time the arguments have to be rehearsed and the conclusions tested.

I meet the bereaved not as someone whose role it is to oversee a rite of passage with as much dignity, thoughtfulness and sensitivity as they have a right to expect, but as another human being who has argued the case on their behalf and will hold their hands with the sincerity of assurance. They may be grateful for, or ignorant of the journey I have made to meet them where they are, but that is not what matters. What counts is that, whether for believer or unbeliever, intimations of immortality have broken through to enable them to regard themselves differently.

Without a perspective that sees everyone as born to pursue a journey that is temporal and eternal, what each does with her or his life in relation to others, to creation, becomes selfish and self centred. If on the other hand now is only the First Act in a longer drama, we will pace ourselves differently from our performance in a one act play, and the long distance runner will have a different game plan to the hundred meter sprinter. It is because we have lost this sense of the larger canvas that our lives have tended to the crabby and short term, and it is spirituality's gift to enable us to recover our original destiny. To pull back from exhausting our planet home of its resources or suffocating it with our waste; to reach out beyond the limitations of our culture in the face of implacable evil; and to build bridges between peoples and faiths. To capture a concept of the hereafter that provides us with a wider, deeper perspective and affects the way we live now; that switches on the light in a dark room and de-mystifies the frightening, shadowy shapes, showing them up for what they really are. Religion is only a lie where spirituality is denied.

But it is not about perspective alone, important though that is. It is also about how we see this 'everyman' that is you and me. It is not ultimately about behaviour, but about being. Once we get the being right the behaviour will follow. It is missing the point to imagine that to live from a perspective of eternity, is not to live wholly in the present, that to be conscious of heaven, we become less real. Rather the reverse. It is because we see our lives as a whole from their origins in the womb to their flowering in the being of God that each part of it, now as well as then, matters. The great world religions all have their way of presenting it and of relating real time to the timelessness of existence. For the Sikh the destiny of every soul is ultimately to go to God, though it may have to pass through successive re-incarnations on the way, depending on the life lived. In Islam Paradise awaits those whom Allah judges to have been faithful on earth. In the Christian story the argument centres on a view of a God whose nature is love, and of humankind destined to find its ultimate fulfilment in a relationship of love with that God.

But bad things happen to good and bad people alike along the way. There is disease, natural and man-made disaster, war, mental and physical cruelty. If this is how it is, and if this is not how it was meant to be, then a God of love must have had in mind a longer time span for humanity than the seventy-one years of Roth's anti-hero, or however many more or less years the rest of us have. The 'slings and arrows of outrageous fortune', 'the heartache and the thousand natural shocks that flesh is heir to' cannot have been a surprise to God! God must have seen it coming! God must have known it was as likely as not to be the consequence of creating free agents in a self regulating universe, that people would do despicable things to each other, illness intrude and cut down, volcanoes erupt and rivers overflow. So God must have intended from the beginning that the life that emerges in flesh and blood, to be thwarted and tested by calamity and suffering, should be a life that continues to be and to grow, when flesh and blood no longer sustain it. This is not wishful thinking or the inability to face up to our mortality, it is the logical consequence of believing in a God of love.

The Christian argument is given a uniquely, outrageously daring twist in claiming that once, in a specific place and at a specific time, this loving God not only lived a life of flesh and blood, but also took issue with the evil consequences of people's free choice. God with us was not to be the charmed life of a god who walks upon the earth impervious to the reality all around, only to withdraw at the end unscathed and unaffected. Jesus, by drawing down on himself the evil consequences of the free choice built into creation, to the extent of being killed as flesh and blood, now invites us all to play out our part in God's circle of love.

When young Paul in 'Dombey and Son' by Charles Dickens lies dying, he whispers to his sister Florence at that moment when he seems to be suspended between the here-and-now and the hereafter: "Mama is like you, Floy. I know her by the face! But tell them that the print upon the stairs at school is not divine enough. The light about the head is shining on me as I go!' It is one of the great death scenes in the whole of English literature. In an age when we are more likely to be at ease with the attitude to death of Philip Roth's anti-hero, we can find Dickens' sentimentality embarrassing, but it reflected a commonly held view then that life didn't end when the heart stopped beating. It was not necessary for Dickens to explain to his readers that the 'print upon the stairs at school' was a portrayal of Jesus, it was part of their culture, a copy maybe of Raphael's 'Transfiguration'?

To our post enlightenment minds the questions that surface in any serious consideration of the hereafter are, What is it? Where is it? And, fundamental to both: Is it? That 'the hereafter' exists as much as 'this earth in time and space exists' is the logical consequence of believing in a God of love, and in what that means in terms of the unfulfilled promises of the lives we all lead. The What and the Where are conceivable when we learn again to think the unthinkable. The Stone Age aborigine may have believed he'd seen a bigger, noisier kookaburra flying over Uluru, but we know it was an aeroplane. Pictures moving and talking on a surface like the shiny page of a book would have been as incomprehensible to Caesar in Rome as to Peter, James and John, but we call it television and don't think twice about it. If God is, then whoever and wherever God is must be unimaginable. But we can imagine enough to realise that our imagination can only take us so far, and that God is both inconceivable but also knowable at one and the same time.

Will we recognise and be recognised? Of course, but better. And who will share this perfection of being with us? Whoever we want who once existed in time and space and who live on now in eternity, as we will be for those who will want us. And everywhere God, God who Christians have seen in the human face of Jesus. The Jews will rejoice with Abraham, the Moslems with Muhammad. The Buddhists with the Buddha. In so far as we can conceive of it here and now there will be something we might recognise as a process of truth and reconciliation, where there will be a profound facing up to wrongs done and a realisation of the cost of acceptance. There will be a completion to our misconceptions about each other and about God, and we will be amazed that we did not see it before, but delighted to realise it at last. It will be a state of endless creation and recreation. Spirituality comes into its own when it holds that both human existence and eternity are equally real, and it is the reality of eternity that transfigures the reality of life on earth, and makes it not just bearable but potentially magnificent.

For some, the drama played out on that mountainside all those years ago took place not in the middle but at the end of Jesus' mission. That it was essentially a resurrection appearance. Perhaps it was both. In the middle it gives intimations of the human reality that's shot through with the divine. At the end it takes earth into the eternity of God, where there is neither religion nor spirituality, only the realisation of faith. But to reach it we need both religion and spirituality, compassionate religion, realistic spirituality.

Trails

The references below are for those interested in wandering off on any of the trails raised by some of the references in different chapters. It is not intended to be an exhaustive list, merely an indication of some of the ideas and sources that have informed my thinking and the themes in this book. The account of the four men who strode out of town, which recurs throughout, can be found in Mark chapter 9, verses 2 to 8, and Matthew chapter 17, verses 1 to 8, in addition to Luke's version, reproduced after the Preface. Branwen's story occurs in the Second Branch of the Mabinogi, in Sioned Davies' translation of the Celtic masterpiece, 'The Mabinogion' (Oxford UP, 2007). The original manuscripts are to be found in the Red Book of Hengest, in the Bodleian Library, Oxford, and in the White Book of Rhydderch, in the National Library of Wales, Aberystwyth. The Mabinogion were first translated into English between 1838 and 1846 by Lady Charlotte Guest.

1. The movement of a curtain: religion's eclipse by spirituality
'Fear wist not' from Francis Thompson's 'The Hound of Heaven'
    (can be read on line)
'To become Christians': Keith Ward in 'Holding Fast to God'
    (SPCK 1982)
Twentieth century wars: BBC 'What the world thinks of God'
    (February 2004)
'Reckless hearts': Psalm 14, verse 1 & Psalm 53, verse 1 (Mgr Knox
    translation)
'What is man?': Psalm 8, verses 4 & 5 (Revised English Bible, 1989
    / REB)
Director of a British and Irish spirituality network: Eley McAinsh
    in a Paper to Union of Monastic Superiors at Ampleforth
    (2007)
R S Thomas: 'Folk Tale' in 'Laboratories of the Spirit' (Macmillan
    1975)

Pantycelyn: quoted by A M Allchin in 'Praise Above All' (UWP 1991)

'I sleep but my heart is awake', etc: Song of Songs chapter 5, verse 2 & chapter 7, verse 7 (REB)

Rostopovich: quoted by Andrew Clark in a Financial Times obituary (28 April 2007)

2. A worse mess: spirituality as religion's inspiration

'I remember, I remember 'from Thomas Hood's 'The house where I was born' (can be read on line)

'Homeless Aramaean': Deuteronomy chapter 26, verse 5 (REB)

The Eucharist: C H Dodd in 'The Founder of Christianity' (MacMillan, 1970)

'Dirty old tramp': Matthew 12: 45 and following (Good as New translation, O Books, 2004)

Ed Husain: 'The Islamist' (penguin 2007)

Charles Taylor: 'A Secular Age' (Harvard University Press, 2007)

Keiji Nakazawa: 'Barefoot Gen – A cartoon history of Hiroshima'

3. Outside both worlds: religion as spirituality's memory

'something religious' from 'Having our Tea' by Bobi Jones in 'Twentieth Century Welsh Poems' translated by Joseph P Clancy (Gomer, 1982)

Rumi, the Sufi poet of love: programme note

Aberlard: 'Heloise and Abelard', by Regine Pernoud (Collins, 1973)

Lord Kumura: 'Love Letters', collected by Antonia Fraser (Weidenfeld and Nicolson, 1976)

Burning Bush: Exodus chapter 3 (REB)

D Densil Morgan: in 'The Span of the Cross' (Univ of Wales Press, 1999)

Gordon Lynch: 'The New Spirituality: Progressive Faith in the 21st century' (Macmillan, 2007)

'Earth's crammed with heaven': from 'Aurora Leigh' by Elizabeth

Barrett Browning (can be read on line)

Joan Puls: 'Seek Treasures in Small Fields' (DLT, 1993)

4. Got no Dreaming?: spirituality as the hope of planet earth

'ah wretch' from the 'Rime of the Ancient Mariner' by Coleridge (can be read on line)

Judas Maccabaeus: I & II Maccabees (REB Apocrypha)

Muta a Murinbata: quoted by Don Carrington in 'The Cultured Pearl' (JBCE, 1986)

Brundtland Commission: 1987 report, 'Our Common Future'

Prospect of world peace: Flannery: Financial Times interview

Creation in need of a human response: see Romans chapter 8, verse 19 following

Namaan: second book of Kings Chapter 5

Hobsbawm: 'The Age of Extremes' (Michael Joseph, 1994)

Four Horsemen: Revelation chapter 6

Extremism: see Nicholas Guyatt: 'Have a Nice Doomsday: Why Millions of Americans Are Looking Forward to the End of the World' (Edbury Press, 2007)

'I am the wind': quoted in 'Celtic Fire' by Robert Van de Weyer (DLT 1990)

Thomas Merton: quoted in 'Praise Above All' by A M Allchin ((Univ Wales Press 1991)

Waldo Williams: 'Knowing', translated by Noel Davies in' God's Family at Worship' (CCW 1986)

Hildergard of Bingen: quoted in 'The Revenge of Gaia' by James Lovelock (penguin, 2006)

Albert Schweitzer: see George Seaver's 'the man and his mind': (Black 1955)

Gwyneth Lewis, National Poet of Wales: July 2007, on BBC Radio 4

Psalms: 8, 24, 65, 121, 148 (REB)

5. An unacknowledged barrier: the helplessness of religion in the face of systemic evil

'The tree of knowledge' and later, 'Mad worshippers': from 'In the Century of the beast' by Alan Llwyd in 'A Welsh Pilgrim's Manual' (Gomer 1989)

Ionescu's play: 'La Lecon' translated as 'The Lesson' (Penguin plays, 1967)

Commotion: Mark chapter 9, verse 14 following (Good as New, 2004)

'The hole in God's side': from 'Roger Bacon' in 'Frequencies' by R S Thomas (Macmillan 1983)

'Share your secret': from 'Pentecost' by Mair Eluned Davies in 'A Welsh Pilgrim's Manual' (above)

'There is death in the pot': second book of Kings, chapter 4, verse 40 (REB, 1989)

'God goeth to every man': Bonhoeffer: Letters and Papers from Prison (Fontana, 1959)

Sheila Cassidy: 'Audacity to Believe' (Collins, 1977)

6. Awareness to awareness: spirituality as the antidote to racism

Barack Obama: a contender for the Democratic Party nomination in the USA at the time of writing. Remarks contained in his speech 'A More Perfect Union'.

'the flame of a force': from 'Judgement of the Black Man' by Kaoberdiano Dambara in 'Poems of Black Africa', edited by Wole Soyinka (Heinemann 1975)

'I pity them greatly': by William Cowper, quoted in 'Bury The Chains' by Adam Hochschild (Pan Books, 2006)

'Genetic biologist': Craig Venter interviewed about his book, ' A Life Decoded, My Genome, My Life' (penguin, 2007)

'The primitive gravity' from Davies Aberpennar / Pennar Davies' poem, translated by Cynthia Davies

Martin Luther King: 'Strength to Believe' (Fontana 1969)

Allan Boesak: 'If this is Treason' (fount 1987)

Joan Puls: 'Seek Treasures in Small Fields' (DLT, 1993)

Wilfred Owen: 'Greater Love' in 'Modern Verse chosen by Phyllis M Jones' (OUP, 1957)

'The child is black': Alan Roberts /Earl Robinson lyric

'More than a science': Rowan Williams in 'The Wound of Knowledge' (DLT, 1979)

Tutu: from 'Hope and Suffering' (Grand Rapids, 1984)

Nationalism: see George McKenna: 'Origins of American Patriotism' (Yale, 2007)

'The black and white': in 'Glas-Nos' by Pennar Davies (CND Cymru, 1987)

7. Walk in the water: to belong is to be free

'I was wounded': Zechariah chapter 13, verse 6 (Revised Version, 1884)

'I must go down': Masefield's 'Sea Fever' (can be read on line)

Roselip's haikus, including 'Listen to Light', can be read on line

Grace Davie: 'Religion in Britain since 1945: Believing without Belonging' (Blackwell,1994)

Talmud story: recounted by Jonathan Sachs in 'To Heal a Fractured World' (Continuum, 2005)

Quakers in Poland: related by Bishop Kenneth Cracknell (source unknown)

'when you were nobody special': from the first letter of Peter chapter 2, verse 9 (Good as New)

8. A freckled world: how ecumenical is God?

'Glory to God': from 'Pied Beauty' by Gerard Manley Hopkins (Modern Verse, 1900-1950, OUP, 1957)

Keith Ward: 'God, Faith & The New Millennium: Christian Belief in an Age of Science' (Oneworld Publications, Oxford, 1998).

Charles Ives: for an example of bands passing each other, listen to 'Holidays Symphony', or to gospel songs from mission halls in the Third Symphony: 'The Camp Meeting',

Michael Taylor: chapter in 'Observations' (BCC 1986)

'Our birth is but a sleep' from 'Ode on Intimations of Immortality from Recollections of Early Childhood' by William Wordsworth (Palgrave: 'The Golden Treasury', Bartleby, 1999)

'yin and yang': from an article by Martin Palmer: (source unknown)

Swami Agnivesh: in 'Secular Spirituality as a Contextual Critique of Religion' (eds Cornel W du Toit and Cedric P Mayson, Research Institute for Theology and Religion University of South Africa, 2006).

9. Hereafter: beyond both religion and spirituality

'Though lovers be lost': from 'And death shall have no dominion' by Dylan Thomas, coupled with 'Do not go gentle': (Collected Poems 1934-1952, Dent, 1974)

Roth: 'Everyman' (Vintage, 2007)

Tony Harrison: 'I believe life ends' (can be read on line)

'Nothing is real': Gwen Cashmore & Joan Puls: 'Clearing the Way' (WCC 1990)

'Desmond and Larry'; Luke chapter 16, verse 19 following (Good as New)

'Wish I's in heaven': spiritual

Sidney Carter: 'Every star shall sing a carol' (100 Hymns for Today, Ancient and Modern, 1972)

Charles Dickens: 'Dombey and Son', chapter 16 'What the waves were always saying' (Oxford Classics, 2001)

Acknowledgements

My thanks to John Hunt for encouraging the idea, to John Henson who did sterling work saving me from numerous errors of omission and commission, to Ray Vincent who spotted mistakes I'd missed, to Andrew Wilson-Dixon who first introduced me to the music of Charles Ives, to Stephen Raw for the perceptive cover design and section illustrations, to the Frink Estate and Yorkshire Sculpture Park for permission to use a detail of Elizabeth Frink's Riace, to Sioned Davies for the quotations from the original Mabinogi, to Gwyneth Lewis for sharing her unpublished Ode, to Eley McAinsh and Greg Barker for inter-faith insights, but especially to my wife, Denise, who supported me throughout and whose suggestions have enriched the text as she has my life. I have no one to blame for the remaining mistakes but myself!

BOOKS

O is a symbol of the world, of oneness and unity. In different cultures it also means the "eye", symbolizing knowledge and insight. We aim to publish books that are accessible, constructive and that challenge accepted opinion, both that of academia and the "moral majority".

Our books are available in all good English language bookstores worldwide. If you don't see the book on the shelves ask the bookstore to order it for you, quoting the ISBN number and title. Alternatively you can order online (all major online retail sites carry our titles) or contact the distributor in the relevant country, listed on the copyright page.

See our website www.o-books.net for a full list of over 400 titles, growing by 100 a year.

And tune in to myspiritradio.com for our book review radio show, hosted by June-Elleni Laine, where you can listen to the authors discussing their books.

MySpiritRadio